Business Networking for Geeks

Copyright © 2024 Richard Tubb. All rights reserved.

Illustrations © Michael de Groot

No part of this document may be reproduced, sold, stored in or introduced into a retrieval system, or transmitted, in any form or by any means (electronic, mechanical, photocopying, recording or otherwise), without the prior permission of the copyright owner.

Disclaimer: The author assumes no responsibility for the use or misuse of this product, or for any injury, damage and/or financial loss sustained to persons or property as a direct or indirect result of using this report. The author cannot guarantee your future results and/or success, as there are some unknown risks in business and on the Internet that we cannot foresee. The use of the information contained in this book should be based on your own due diligence, and you agree that the author is not liable for any success or failure of your business that is directly or indirectly related to the purchase and use of this information.

First printing: 2024

ISBN-13: 9798325825149

British Cataloguing Publication Data:
A catalogue record of this book is available from The British Library.

Also available on Kindle.

Business Networking for Geeks

Richard Tubb

Contents

Foreword 7
Introduction 10
Common Objections to Business Networking 14
Tactics: Before You Go to an Event...16
Tactics: At the Networking Event...23
Learning to be a Natural Networker 34
Tactics: After the Networking Event 37
Making Business Introductions...50
Why You Should Use Social Networking for Business (If You Don't Already)..58
Business Networking on LinkedIn 70
Business Networking on Twitter 80
Using Social Networking to Listen to Customer Feedback 84
Business Networking at Virtual Events 89
Business Networking is a Skill 98
Bringing Your Clients Together Through Networking 100
Digital Business Card Apps to Make Networking and Follow-ups Easier..105
The Importance of Peer Groups 109
IT Conferences and Their Importance to Your Business 119
Conclusion...124
Business Networking Event Cheat Sheet...126
Acknowledgements 128

Foreword

People often think about business networking purely in terms of meeting people they can sell to. After all, even if you've never attended them we're all familiar with the sort of events where, typically over breakfast, everyone stands up and, in 60 seconds, tells you why you should buy from them.

Plenty of people – and, I daresay, a number of IT professionals – think networking isn't for them. They might not need new clients, or they feel there is a better route to market.

So, before you read this book, I want to challenge that a little.

Business networking is a massive route to market for so many businesses and business owners, if handled correctly. But it can be so much more, and so valuable to you and your business. If you bear with me, I'll explain.

Firstly, if you learn how to do it properly, networking – both in real life and on social media – can result in new business, and referrals from the folks who grow to know, like and trust you.

The more you get to know people, the more they get to know you and your business, the more you'll be the first person they think of when one of their clients or contacts has an IT issue that you might be able to help with.

After many years of networking and after meeting thousands of people I am constantly asked if I know someone who does this or can sort that out and, of course, I make an introduction to someone I trust who does what the person is looking for.

Networking can be your route into businesses you want to approach but don't know how, and to new markets you hadn't considered. If the local accountant, solicitor, commercial agent, architect or any number of businesses gets to know you, you're more likely to be referred when one of their customers is moaning that they haven't been able to do their accounts because their network is down, or they're struggling with their staff working remotely these days, or whatever it happens to be.

Secondly, we all have specialities and business networking has enabled me to go for jobs I would previously have had to turn down. By talking to other folk who sell to the same market as me, I've been able to put together collaborations and loose joint ventures when asked for services I sort of provide, but that aren't my core offering.

So, by collaborating with a sales trainer, I've been able to put together courses based on how to find customers through networking, with my collaborator talking about how to close the business.

By collaborating with a PR expert, I've been able to offer more services to the folk I train to speak, to help them actually find speaking gigs.

Therefore, if you're an IT Managed Service Provider focused on infrastructure, you could collaborate with a telecoms specialist. If you're an expert on IT security, you could collaborate with a hardware supplier – and help both of you win more business.

Networking helps you get to know other business folk and decide if you trust them enough to collaborate with them.

Thirdly, the support I've had from networking over the years as I've grown my reputation and my business has been invaluable. The opportunity to chat with folks in an informal setting about the aspects of business that I'm not good at has allowed me to benefit from advice and to choose suppliers who I have got to know and trust (that phrase again) over time. If my week is going badly, I can go to a networking event and be cheered up and inspired by some of the other folk in the (sometimes virtual) room; if my week is going well, there's a group of people who will cheer me on and allow me my moment of showing off.

Richard Tubb 'gets' networking. From the moment I met him we've kept in touch, enjoying our infrequent face to face meetings, but chatting in the background over social networking. Not only does Richard understand how networking works, he understands how it works for IT professionals and, therefore, how it can work for you.

In a nod to what I've already mentioned in this foreword, over the eight years or so since I met Richard, he decided he liked me and trusted me enough to ask me to write this piece for his book (which is extremely flattering) and I knew I liked him and trusted him enough to do it.

Geeks, get networking. With Richard's guidance you can make it successful for you and your business. Keep this book somewhere you can refer to it often. I know so many of you will find it, and networking, a vital part of your armoury.

Stefan Thomas
Author of Business Networking for Dummies
stefanthomas.biz

Introduction

When we talk about business networking, what images does it conjure up for you?

Struggling to remember elevator pitches? Making small talk with complete strangers?

Typically, business networking is something most of us don't look forward to.

For me – a typical geek who was more interested in sitting behind a keyboard talking to computers than talking to human beings – the idea of walking into a room full of strangers and selling myself or my products and solutions to them brought me out in a cold sweat.

However, when I ran my own IT Managed Service Provider (MSP) business, I quickly realised you can be the best IT company in the world, but if nobody knows about you, what is the point?

Therefore, getting out there to business networking events and connecting with people online was an essential part of growing my business.

However, what I learned was that there's a lot more to networking than awkwardly trying to shake hands whilst holding a coffee and a greasy bacon sandwich.

Neither is networking all about selling yourself or your business to others.

Effective networking is about building relationships where work opportunities happen naturally, not from enforced business card swapping. And effective networking happens in more places than you'd realise.

While those traditional 'face to face chat and business card swap' events still go on, modern business owners also network online, at conferences, training sessions and even in their personal lives.

Whenever you introduce a colleague or acquaintance to someone you think would be helpful to them, that's networking.

When you bring like-minded people together to talk business or mastermind, that's networking.

My own journey into business networking allowed me to realise that the best business owners know it's not just about winning clients for themselves. It's about building relationships, helping each other out, getting yourself known and learning new things all the time.

This book is based on many years of pushing myself out of my comfort zone and learning how to enjoy business networking events.

Throughout those years, I wrote blog posts, sharing with the world what had worked (and what hadn't worked!) for me in business, including my experience of business networking.

I sold my MSP business a number of years ago now, but I still use what I learned about business networking while attending and speaking at conferences and events all over the world.

Despite this learning and my networking experiences, I still never considered myself a proficient business networker.

Then something funny happened.

Some years ago, after moving from my hometown of Birmingham to Newcastle-upon-Tyne in the north east of England, I attended my first business networking event in this new area.

Now, it can be nerve-wracking enough to walk into a room full of strangers. But to walk into a room full of strangers in a strange new city... Eek!

Despite my years of attending networking events, I felt vulnerable and out of place.

Thankfully, my friend and colleague Gudrun Lauret saw me looking lost and took pity on me. Gudrun introduced me to people, acted as a great connector and generally demonstrated excellence at business networking.

After a while of witnessing this, I asked Gudrun: "Where did you learn to become a good networker?"

Gudrun laughed and surprised me by telling me, "I read your blog posts!"

I guess the old adage is true. We teach that which we most need to learn.

Now I still get nervous when I walk into a room full of strangers. But I know that if I rely on what I've learned (and what you are about to learn in this book) there is nothing to worry about.

And so, the idea for this book was born. The goal? To collate all the networking experiments I'd documented in my blog posts and share them with the world.

As a result, this book is designed as a resource for IT professionals, Managed Service Providers (MSPs), IT Solution Providers and any other techies who are looking to make better connections, find collaborators and, ultimately, do more business.

And when I say techies, I do, of course, mean geeks.

I speak as a fully-fledged card-carrying geek who has learned that technical ability will take you so far, but the ability to be a connector and build a network of high value contacts will propel you far beyond where you could go alone.

But don't just take my word for it!

Throughout this book, I've asked some of the world's top business networkers to contribute their thoughts and ideas. Every one of these contributors is an IT business owner, just like you. You can find these golden nuggets in the boxes interspersed within every chapter.

My hope is that this book allows you to learn that mastering business networking allows you to elevate yourself from plain, run-of-the-mill, technically brilliant but socially awkward geek, to the geek that everyone wants to know.

Common Objections to Business Networking

Since selling my IT business, I do a lot of work helping the owners of other IT businesses to avoid the many mistakes I made during my time as an MSP.

One of the common questions I'm asked by business owners is: "How do I find new clients?"

While marketing tactics such as direct mail, telesales and email blasts do have a huge part to play in finding new clients, used in isolation these tactics nearly always fail.

What is more, the majority of MSPs find it difficult to be consistent with their marketing efforts. As I am fond of saying, marketing is a process, not an event!

Therefore, my answer to finding new clients always begins with telling MSPs to get out there and meet fellow businesses by attending networking events.

Attending events to meet new people, build new relationships and strengthen existing relationships is very important. I'd say it should be an integral part of any IT Solution Provider or MSP's marketing plans.

But the push-back I often get when I recommend networking is:

- "We've tried networking, and it doesn't work for us."
- "We meet the wrong people."
- "It's a waste of my time."
- "I've nothing in common with the people I meet."

These are all common complaints I hear from IT businesses about networking events. And I understand this attitude because I've been there myself!

Dragging yourself up at the crack of dawn to attend a networking breakfast that feels like a waste of time. Pushing yourself to attend the latest Chamber meeting where people seem more interested in talking about their sports teams than business.

But participating in business networking *does* work.

You can meet the right people who you *can* do business with – either directly or indirectly. And attending in-person business networking events doesn't have to be a chore.

> Business networking is not the natural habitat for techs who much prefer to stay in the backroom and communicate via email. I have bravely ventured out into the world of networking!
>
> Suzanne Rice, Computer Troubleshooters

Tactics: Before You Go to an Event

A common objection to business networking events is that they are stressful to attend. The IT industry is full of introverted folk who prefer talking to computers to spending time with human beings!

If you're anything like me, you may find organised networking events stressful and nerve-wracking. Therefore, you may actively avoid them whenever possible.

However, the more you attend these events, the easier it gets – and it's good to remember that a lot of the other attendees will be feeling the same way as you!

One tactic I'd suggest you use to make networking easier is to consider what you want to get out of the event, rather than just rock up and hope for the best! It is very useful to think about what your objectives are *before* you arrive. As a result of being prepared and having a clear goal, you will be more relaxed about the meeting.

Here are my three top tips for making sure you get the most out of the networking events you attend.

Choose the Right Event

Choosing the right networking event to go to is key. But how will you know the right event to attend?

Firstly, there is likely to be much more networking running in your area than you could imagine. A quick web search for 'business networking near me' should reveal all sorts of events.

I'd also recommend checking out sites such as Eventbrite and Meetup.com, which will help you find networking events aimed at specific niches: small businesses near you, IT professionals, and even technology user groups (more on the value of networking with your peers later in this book!).

Searching for events in this way should give you an idea of what is available for you to attend.

However, rather than randomly signing up for an event you've found via Google, Eventbrite or Meetup, why not ask your clients, business partners such as suppliers and contractors, and other business owners which events they attend and find useful.

Your friends, colleagues, clients and suppliers are likely to be able to point you in the right direction. Perhaps they'll even invite you to join them at the next event they are attending.

Knowing somebody at an event also has the bonus of meaning they can introduce you to others when you are there.

While there's no guarantee that the events others recommend will be an ideal fit for you, experience tells me that a recommendation from others is a much better way to choose where and when to spend your time than picking the first event that pops up in a web search.

> Of late, I make others in the business ALSO do business networking. It is pointless if I am the only person the business community knows, as once I have retired, that link is broken. So, our Business Development Manager has a seat in a BNI chapter now. I did it 15 years ago; he needs to build his network now.
>
> David Brereton, Myson Pages

Check Out the Attendee List Prior to the Meeting

One of the tactics I learned early on in my networking journey was to attend events with a *purpose in mind*. Sure, rocking up at an event and seeing what happens can be fun – but if you're a nervous networker, that uncertainty will only add to your discomfort.

So, I always set a purpose for my business networking.

That purpose could be that I wanted to be introduced to somebody with a certain skillset. Or perhaps I wanted to meet a specific type of business owner.

Once I'd got a purpose in mind, it became useful for me to understand whether the event could help me meet the right people.

To this day, I'm still surprised by the number of attendees at business networking events who don't bother to research who else is attending the event.

After all, if you don't know who is attending, how can you know whether you're going to be able to meet the right people or not?

Having blind hope that I'd meet the right people never seemed like a very effective way of meeting my goals.

In my experience, most progressive business networking events publish an attendee list prior to the event to allow everyone to see who is attending.

It's always a good idea to scan the attendee list and try to find out more about the other people who are going to the event.

Once you're armed with some knowledge of who you can expect to meet, you can then effectively consider which people in the room you would like to *personally* meet.

Perhaps you will spot people you've already heard of, or folks who might be in a similar industry to you. It could be there are a number of people attending who may be ideal clients.

And knowing who you want to meet at an event is preferable to turning up and hoping you bump into somebody with whom you have something in common!

> For those looking to build their network, I would say this. A) Start with people you know and trust, then work to be introduced to people they know. If you know someone YOU trust, then they will likely know other similar people. B) Ensure you understand what people in your network do and what they're looking for, so you can keep your eyes open for opportunities. Finally, C) Always put in 2x the effort to opportunities that come via someone in your network. They've put themselves on the line to recommend you, so go the extra mile and make sure you give that opportunity all you can as it's cost you nothing to receive.
>
> Craig Sharp, Abussi

Even if the attendee list isn't published prior to the event, when you arrive at the venue there's often a list or sign-in sheet, or you can ask the event organiser if you can check who is attending. Most event organisers will be happy to share.

Of course, make it clear that you're not simply looking to harvest an attendee list for sales or email marketing purposes – or else you're likely to be discouraged with a 'data protection'-style excuse!

Finally, it's worth remembering that many people announce their attendance at events on social media prior to the event. Check out LinkedIn groups and run Twitter searches for keywords related to your networking event to see if you can find other attendees, and then seek them out on the day itself.

Which leads us nicely to my final tip related to your pre-event activities.

> Computer Troubleshooters enjoys being a member of Sevenoaks Chamber of Commerce. Sevenoaks Chamber is more about making connections with the local business community, but each member can choose how much they wish to put in or take out – no three-line whips, no referrals, no 60-second presentations. The serendipity of who you may meet all adds to the fun, with First Wednesday regularly attracting more than 60 attendees.
>
> Suzanne Rice, Computer Troubleshooters

Announce You're Attending the Event on Social Media

I can't tell you the number of networking events I've attended where I've announced I'm attending on my social media feeds – such as LinkedIn, Twitter and Facebook – and somebody at the event has sought me out to say hello to because they knew I was attending. I've even (flatteringly) had people tell me they'd seen I was going, and so decided to come along too!

Remember that most people feel nervous walking into a room full of strangers, so, by announcing your intention to visit the event on social media, you're doing two positive things:

1. You're giving the event a plug to ensure that more people are aware of it (which the event organisers will be pleased with!)

2. You're giving others the opportunity and excuse to seek you out at the event itself.

You might also find that by announcing your attendance at an event, others – even those who didn't attend – ask you about your experience or tell you they'd like to join you next time.

I'll share more about the power of online networking in a later chapter!

> You are bombarded with opportunities to meet up and you could spend your whole day progressing from one meeting to the next. You clearly have to allow time to work on your business too, although networking is not just a *jolly chat* but is actually a marketing activity.
>
> My preference is to be selective. My main focus currently is on Sevenoaks Chamber, but I am open to occasional events hosted by local companies. I also attend Sevenoaks Voluntary Forum as this brings together representatives from our niche: charities.
>
> Suzanne Rice, Computer Troubleshooters

Summary

In this chapter, we've explored the tactics you can use before a business networking event to ensure you get the most from your attendance.

- Choose the right event. Use web searches, Eventbrite and Meetup.com to research local events and then ask your existing contacts which events they'd recommend.
- Set your intention for the event. Check out the attendee list before you go to find people you want to speak with.
- Announce you're attending the event on social media sites.

> This will help you meet new people when you're networking.

So, now you've found the best networking event to go to, what can you do to make sure you get the most out of it?

In the next chapter, I'll share some tips for 'working the room'.

Tactics: At the Networking Event

> Networking is about making connections, not about selling. No one likes to be sold to or lectured and you will soon get a reputation as a *hunter* if you persist in this behaviour.
>
> You may be feeling shy or nervous as you enter a room full of strangers but remember that the majority of attendees probably feel the same way.
>
> Be brave and go over to talk to someone you don't know – they are likely to be very grateful you made the first move. Also, there's nothing worse than being confronted with a roomful of cliques, where you feel you are excluded from the conversation. Don't be that person who only chats with their friends; be open and welcoming to new contacts.
>
> Suzanne Rice, Computer Troubleshooters

I've had a lot of success attending conferences and dedicated networking events, but as I shared earlier, I've had to get over my fear of meeting new people. To this day, I find this part of business networking difficult and even now the idea of a room full of strangers will sometimes have me breaking out into a cold sweat!

However, by using the tactics I shared in the last chapter and preparing for the event before attending, you can put some nerves to rest by setting your expectations of who you will meet and what you will talk to them about.

Still, when I attend business networking events, I have a habit of finding one familiar face and then just talking to that person!

Falling into this trap of spending all your time having the same conversations with someone you already know can leave you feeling as though you've wasted an opportunity to meet new people.

Or, worse, you can be 'that person' who stands in the corner of the room, desperately pretending to be busy on their smartphone so they can avoid talking to anyone. (If this hits a nerve, don't worry – I've done it too!)

Over the years though, I've picked up a few techniques to help me step outside my comfort zone, meet new people and feel comfortable in conversation.

Therefore, here are four ways to 'work the room'.

Look for an Open Conversation

When you're looking for a conversation, look for an 'open' group you can join, not a 'closed' one.

A closed group is where two people are facing each other straight on, or a group of people have formed an inward-facing circle and are talking intently. These groups have something important to discuss and are focused entirely on each other.

Don't be that person who hovers nearby, helplessly looking for a gap in the conversation so you can introduce yourself. That gap in the conversation might be a long time coming!

Instead, seek out an open conversation. This is where two or more people are chatting and standing in an open semi-circle – subconsciously inviting someone else to join them.

The conversation in this circle is not intense and you'll find that either there will be a lull in their chat, where you can easily introduce yourself, or, just as likely, somebody else in the group will smile and introduce themselves to you.

> Get out there, say hello and ask questions – open-ended ones. Lots of people at networking events are looking to talk about themselves and get to know people. Let them! Asking open-ended questions gives them a chance to update you. You'll get your chance by return, but you won't come across as someone who is looking for a quick sell. Quick sells lead to customers who are short term. Build a relationship and a presence and they will come.
>
> David Brereton, Myson Pages

Politely Interrupt Conversations

If you followed my advice and prepared for the event before attending, you're almost certainly going to have some people in the room you actively want to seek out and speak to. However, when you get to the event and spot them, they might be popular and part of a closed circle or engaged in a one-to-one conversation.

Again, there is no need to hover around waiting for a moment to speak to them. Instead, in my experience, people don't mind a brief interruption in their conversation to acknowledge you.

I typically politely interrupt the conversation with an apology to all parties involved, and then quickly let the individual know who I am and that I'd love to speak with them later. I then apologise again for the interruption and tell everyone that I'll let them get on.

In my experience, rather than being seen as rude, people fully understand that this is a business networking event with lots of people involved.

And sometimes, the person I've wanted to speak to will use the interruption as an excuse to extract themselves from a conversation to come and join me immediately!

Remember, other people may be waiting to meet you, too!

> Attendees are there to network, so you have permission to talk to them about your business and to approach people you don't know, as long as they are not clearly involved in a private conversation. Connect, engage with them and ask interesting questions (you can prepare some conversation openers in advance). Only once you have established a connection should you mention your company and the type of professions you would like to link up with – your niche.
>
> Suzanne Rice, Computer Troubleshooters

Make It All About Them

Once you've struck up a conversation with somebody, what do you say beyond small talk?

Well, it's worth remembering that everyone's favourite topic is themselves! Who doesn't like to talk about themself, right?

Therefore, when meeting someone, try to resist the urge to talk about yourself and instead use the opportunity to learn about the other people by asking questions about them.

'Small talk' is fine – where they travelled from, have they attended this group or event before and so on – but consider asking them what they're looking for from the day or session.

This is particularly good at a conference – ask them what they are looking forward to on the agenda, and what impact they hope it will have on their business.

As well as learning more about them and their business, you may find you have a lot in common or even learn something about yourself.

Be the Connector

One tactic I've found particularly satisfying (and powerful) at a business event is focusing on 'being the connector'.

So, what does being a connector mean?

Well, during your chat with somebody, and throughout the event or conference as a whole, look for opportunities to introduce people to one another based on commonality.

For instance, for those of us attending IT conferences, if one person tells you they specialise in Voice-Over-IP (VoIP) and another tells you they are looking to get into providing VoIP solutions to their clients – connect them up!

Or the next time you're at a Managed Services event and a peer shares that they are currently implementing a Professional Services Automation (PSA) tool, and another shares they are considering or just beginning to implement a PSA tool – connect the two parties!

> The most important fact when networking is to **smile** and tell stories. Never try and sell to the room; sell through the room.
>
> If you try to sell to the person in the room, that's one contact.
>
> If you sell through the room (by telling a good/happy story), the one contact will probably repeat the story to 10+ others.
>
> Using Pareto's Law, talk for 20% of the time, ask the right questions and listen for 80%.
>
> Again, if you ask the right questions and are willing to learn, the person is more likely to remember you. If you 'pitch' to someone without knowing them, they'll more likely try to avoid you at the next networking event.
>
> Robert Gibbons, IT Expert

This might sound like common sense, but by training yourself to keep your antennae up and looking for opportunities to connect people, you become very valuable to everyone around you.

By looking for opportunities to be the connector and introduce people to one another, you'll be adding value to every conversation you have and every relationship you form.

What's more, it's human nature to try to reciprocate!

As a result of this tendency in humans to want to repay favours, don't be surprised if those same people find you during the day, at a conference or the next time you meet, and introduce you to people that they think *you* will find valuable to know.

Focusing on being the connector was a tactic that changed my attitude to networking events from being something I felt was a chore into being something I really enjoyed. Try it. It may work for you, too!

And if the idea of being a connector inspires you, I highly recommend you check out the wonderful book *The Go-Giver: A Little Story About a Powerful Business Idea* by Bob Burg and John David-Mann.

The Go-Giver expands upon this concept of providing value to others and is powerful reading for anyone who wants to take their business networking (and life skills) to the next level.

> 'Networking' translates differently based on the country where it occurs: Italy is more successful when there is a neutral catalyst, provided that meetings won't be 'salesy', which is something many people still fear.
>
> Vera Tucci, T-Consulting

When the Conversation Ends

Now, we've all been in those conversations with strangers when the chat runs out of steam and an awkward silence falls.

It's cringeworthy, isn't it?

So, what do you do when the conversation runs its course?

Well, if and when the conversation runs to its inevitable conclusion, you are both left with that awkward silence and it seems like there is nothing more to say, you could of course excuse yourself and make a beeline for the toilet.

Or you could answer a phantom mobile phone call from 'the office' (the close cousin of the 'stand in the corner and pretend to read emails on my smartphone' we mentioned earlier).

However, when the conversation comes to a natural end, you could avoid all that awkwardness and use this phrase instead:

"I'd imagine you know a few people here?"

If the answer from the other person comes back "Yes" then share with them that you don't know many people and you'd find it really valuable if they wouldn't mind introducing you to some new people.

In this way, you're giving the other person the opportunity to be the connector themselves!

> By focusing on one to three sprout-sized actions, you can reduce your sense of overwhelm and give your mind something concrete to do during a networking event.
>
> Keep the conversation going – but how could you do this?
>
> - Sprout 1: Make the conversation about them.
>
> Focus on what they are saying – and listen. Ask questions to develop your understanding of what they do and what they are looking for.
>
> - Sprout 2: Slow down and be okay with pauses and silence.
>
> This can take practise but sometimes taking a pause and allowing space can open up a question for you or more explanation from them.
>
> - Sprout 3: when asked what you do, have a pre-prepared sentence or two.
>
> Dave Algeo, Networking Wingman and Restless Midlifer

If the answer comes back "No" and they don't know anyone then nod and share that you're in the same boat and suggest that perhaps you both go and meet someone together.

You could then look to be the connector and introduce them to somebody you already know.

If you do this, take the time to introduce the two people by name and briefly explain to each what the other does and how you know them.

"David, this is Sarah. Sarah was explaining to me how she works in HR. Sarah, David runs a small business so he knows the potential headaches of HR!"

Alternatively, if you don't spot anybody you recognise, you can use the earlier technique we discussed of looking for an individual or open group of people to introduce to your new contact.

> Sell yourself and your culture, but don't sell the tech. The tech continually comes and goes, but you want your MSP business to be a reliable partner to your client. Sell the relationship first; build trust and confidence.
>
> David Brereton, Myson Pages

Summary

In this chapter, we've explored how attending business networking can have a positive impact on your business, but how it does also require you to step outside your comfort zone and face a room full of strangers.

- Avoid falling into the trap of chatting with the same group of people that you already know.

- Be brave and start a conversation with someone new or ask for an introduction to someone you don't yet know.

- Focus on people and ask them about themselves. This puts the other person at ease and helps you both find common ground.

- Look for opportunities to 'be the connector'. When you act as a connector, you'll add value to the conversations you are having with people and make it easy to build new relationships.

I hope this chapter has helped provide you with some solid yet easy to implement tactics to make attending networking events more productive and fun for you.

But what if you're still feeling nervous and you're intimidated by the people in the room chatting, laughing and arranging business meetings?

If you think: "They're natural at networking, they know just the right thing to say and when," then worry not – you too can look like you were born to network!

Further Reading

- *The Go-Giver: A Little Story About a Powerful Business Idea* by Bob Burg and John David-Mann.
- https://tubb.co/recommendedbooks

Learning to be a Natural Networker

We all know those people to whom networking seems to come naturally. The extroverts who are the life and soul of the event. Or those highly respected, influential connectors who seem to know everybody in the room.

But how do they do this? Are they born this way?

Well, I believe some people find it easier to take on certain roles, but in the majority of cases, the individual involved has worked hard to make sure they appear to be a 'natural'. In my experience, this is especially true of what people classify as 'soft skills' – the ability to talk to people, empathise with them, bond with others and so on.

As I've said before, I was a nervous networker in the early days. However, I realised that attending those events was an effective way to grow my IT business and, as a result, I actively sought out learning techniques for becoming more comfortable in those situations.

I read books on the topic of personal confidence and forced myself to stretch my comfort zone by attending more business networking events. My attendance at these events enabled me to practise the techniques I've already shared in this book.

What is more, attending events gave me the opportunity to observe others I considered 'naturals' in the area of networking. In fact, when I came across someone who I admired for clearly being very comfortable in those situations I asked them for advice so I could learn the art of it!

Amusingly, nearly everyone I've ever met who I thought was a natural at networking and asked for advice has confided in me that actually, they find those events quite uncomfortable too, and they have to force themselves to do it.

That's reassuring, isn't it? Nobody is born a natural, and everybody has to learn how to step outside their comfort zone.

So, the next time you see a great natural speaker, effective salesman, connector or influencer, or even someone chatting away effortlessly at the coffee table, remember they have probably worked hard on that skill to be able to give the impression they are a 'natural' at these things.

I'd encourage you not to dismiss your own potential. Nor should you convince yourself that you're not as gifted as those people you admire.

Instead, turn that assumption on its head and realise that, whether you feel like a natural or not, with the right focus and determination you can become amazing at anything! Reassure yourself that even if those naturals you meet don't feel nervous now, they did feel nervous not so long ago.

I want to share one final thought on the time and energy you invest in becoming a better business networker.

The skills and confidence you pick up on your networking journey will deliver you rewards outside of networking events! For example, I've found that by learning to be the connector, I've become a better salesperson and someone who is always focused on delivering value to others.

Likewise, I've experienced that by learning to show an interest and listen to others at networking events, I've become a better friend, husband and employer. After all, listening is a vastly underrated skill.

Therefore, the time you invest in learning these skills should be seen as an *investment in yourself.*

> **Getting More Personal.** Every MSP or IT service provider sells just one thing first, and that is trust. While it is true that small business owners do business with folks they like, when it comes to critical choices for professional services, including accounting and legal services, and IT support, trust is the coin of the realm. Without trust, you cannot build a relationship.
>
> The first step to building that trust is to find a way to build a bond with someone, often over a shared interest. One of the hardest things about the pandemic was the loss of personal contact and the challenges of trying to build initial trust in its absence. For example, how will you know he loves football if you cannot see his wall of photos? Finding common ground is everything.
>
> Getting naked (in the Pat Lencioni sense) and presenting our own UPIs (unique personalities and interests) is key here.
>
> For me, it's languages, photography, dogs and travel. Figure out what your own UPIs are and use them to bridge that initial 'trust gulf'. You will not connect with everyone, but you will with those who trust you, which is who we want as clients.
>
> Joshua Liberman, Net Sciences

So, we've covered some tips for preparing for the event, and attending the event itself.

Next, you'll find yourself leaving the meeting with a lot of new connections, and probably a stack of business cards that your new acquaintances have shared with you. So, what should you do with all those new contacts?

Tactics: After the Networking Event

It's easy to lose sight of the fact that business networking doesn't end when everyone leaves the event. What do you do with all those new names, faces and business cards you've taken away with you?

You may have good intentions, but often business cards end up at the bottom of a handbag or in a coat pocket. Likewise, new business contacts can end up being neglected with no further contact made.

This diminishes the effort you've put into attending the event and stepping outside your comfort zone to speak to new people.

So, what exactly should you do with all those new business cards you return to the office with?

I have the memory span of a goldfish and often forget the names of people I have spoken to but, after years of going to events, conferences and meetings, I've developed a follow-up routine. The tactics I'll share in this chapter help me remember people more effectively, and I hope you'll find them useful too.

Create Memory Hooks on Business Cards

I don't know about you, but I'm not the best when it comes to remembering faces. I often used to experience the embarrassment of not being able to put a name to a face. However, over the years I've dramatically improved my ability to remember people by using what are known as memory hooks.

In your case, there's a real danger that, however interesting the people you meet at a networking event are, by the time you leave the event, you've forgotten their name or your conversations with them.

Oh, and it's also quite common that they'll have forgotten you too when you go to follow up with them later!

That's why it makes sense to create some memory hooks, for both you and them.

My tip? Take a pen to these events. In fact, take a few – they make handy gifts for your new friends, who will undoubtedly have forgotten (or given away!) their own pen. Then, whenever you receive a business card from someone, on the back of the card make a quick note of one (or more) of three things.

Firstly, make a brief note of **where you met**.

I can't tell you how frustrating it can be to look at a business card and wonder, "Where on earth did I meet this person?!"

Making a note of where you met will create a powerful memory hook for you to recall much more about your new contact.

Secondly, if you're able to, make a brief note of **what you talked**

about.

You probably discussed business, but as we know, people do business with people they know, like and trust. Therefore, your conversation could have been about your shared love of a sports team, a good book you've read recently, or even somebody else you mutually know.

Either way, make a note of your conversation. Even if you don't remember the person's name, you'll probably recall the conversation you had, which will jog your memory about other details.

Finally, make sure to write down on the business card **any commitments you made** during your conversation.

As somebody with a poor memory, I can tell you there's no worse way to start a relationship with somebody new than to casually promise them something and then fail to deliver because you've forgotten to follow up.

For instance, if your conversation highlights an interesting article you've read recently, which your new contact is interested in, write a reminder to send them that article.

Likewise, if you've said you can introduce your new contact to someone else it would be useful for them to meet, make a note of it.

Either way, once you've written a reminder on their business card, make good on your commitment.

First impressions count, and effectively following up on your commitments is a great way to make a good first impression regardless of whether you're a memory master or a goldfish like me.

Don't Let Business Cards Gather Dust

So, you've come back from the networking event. Now what?

Well, if you're like any other typical geek, you'll dump those new business cards you've gathered onto your desk before jumping into your email, checking out new support tickets or listening to voicemails.

Before you know it, it's time for the next networking event and you've not even followed up on your new contacts from the last one!

Then the thought occurs to you, "What if I bump into some of the same people at this new event? How do I explain to them why I've not followed up with them / connected them with that person I promised to connect them with / sent them that article I mentioned?

"Eek! Perhaps I shouldn't bother going to this next event after all..."

It doesn't take much of an excuse to persuade nervous networkers to cancel their attendance at an event, so to eliminate this type of friction, I want you to get organised!

Please don't let those business cards gather dust on your desk. To do so means all the effort you put into meeting new people will be hampered by your inability to follow up effectively.

Instead, before going to any event, I want you to schedule time in your diary **after the event** to process business cards and follow up with people.

For instance, when I schedule a business event in my calendar, I also schedule an appointment with myself for some follow-up time. Typically, within 48 hours of returning from the event, I will have made time to process the business cards I collected and follow up effectively with my new contacts.

Working in the IT industry, it's all too easy to return to your desk and get overwhelmed by emails, phone calls and tickets. By making an appointment with yourself, you know you'll have the time to process those new contacts and set yourself up for success in these new relationships.

Finally, a pro tip for following up.

If you don't already use a Customer Relationship Management (CRM) platform, it may be worth investing in one.

At its very basic level, Outlook Contacts or Google Contacts gives you the ability to make notes for a contact.

When you're processing business cards, make sure to use these notes to remind yourself of where you met the person, what you talked about, and any other pertinent details.

If you have a CRM system, you can make similar notes as well as set reminders to follow up and, if the new contact is a potential client, work through your sales process, too.

In a later chapter, I'll share more details of the tools and systems you can use to effectively process business cards and new contact details.

However, before you get excited at the thought of some new tech and go rushing off to research a shiny new CRM system, remember that for many MSPs, you already have a CRM system that you probably don't use. Your Professional Services Automation (PSA) or Helpdesk platform probably has some built-in CRM functionality.

Regardless of which method you use – a simple note, your PSA, or a CRM system – remember to record your new contact details in your system and follow up effectively.

Next, we'll look at what that follow-up process looks like.

How to Effectively Follow Up with People You've Met

There's no point meeting people, pressing the flesh and exchanging business cards if you don't follow up effectively!

Elaborating on my previous point, if you make a strong connection with someone then I'd encourage you to follow up with an email and remind them where you met and what you discussed. Remember, they may need a memory hook to be reminded of you, too.

A typical email I send to people might be something like:

> Hi, <firstname>,
>
> Great to meet you at <event>. I really enjoyed chatting to you about <topic>. Thanks for making me feel welcome.
>
> As promised, here's a link to the article I mentioned <or> here's the details of the contact I mentioned who you might be interested in meeting.
>
> P.S. Are there any other events you'd recommend to me?

In this type of email, we remind the person where we met and what we spoke about. This type of memory hook is very useful if the other person has attended lots of events recently and met lots of people!

Next, we follow through on any commitments we made during our conversation.

If you've promised to make an introduction, fire up LinkedIn or a new email as soon as you've sent the message to your new contact and do it. That way, you won't forget.

This type of follow-through on your commitment is a strong indicator to your new contact that you are somebody who doesn't just talk the talk but can be trusted to do what they say.

Once you've sent the email, I'd recommend you also connect with the person on LinkedIn. There's more on how to do this effectively in a later chapter.

While emails along the lines I've suggested are fine for following up, in the next section I want to explore a very simple yet underutilised technology that will make you stand out in a sea of networking connections.

Use Video Messaging

How you follow-up with your new contacts will determine whether you become someone memorable to them – a person that sticks in their mind -- or just another forgettable name in a contact list or address book.

Think about it. An email saying "Great to meet you at the event. Let's stay in touch" hardly burns you into memory with your new contact, does it?

Instead, I want you to consider how you can be memorable with your follow-ups.

I'm fond of saying "It's remarkably easy to be remarkable" and when it comes to post-event follow-up messages, there's one very simple way you can be remarkable in your approach.

You can be remarkable by using video.

Nowadays, video is everywhere. You only have to think of the amount of hours lost scrolling through social media to realise video is something people love to consume.

Yet strangely, video isn't used very often in one-to-one business messages.

So, if you sent a video message to follow up with someone you met at a networking event, you'd definitely stand out in an inbox full of emails!

There are tools that make it so simple to send video messages. For example, I use a tool called Hippo Video, which allows me to hit a button within my email client and quickly record a video message via my webcam. When I've finished recording, Hippo Video produces a lovely animated GIF of my video message and inserts it into my email. I click send, and whoosh! The video message flies off to my contact.

(Top tip: when you start recording your video message, wave at the screen. That way, your animated GIF will show some movement rather than just a static image of yourself staring at a camera.)

I consistently get feedback from my contacts that a video message has made their day. After all, such a video is personalised, innovative and, frankly, remarkable in comparison to the sea of boring emails people otherwise receive.

I learned to use video messages effectively when I worked alongside Nigel Moore, the illustrious leader of the Tech Tribe, an awesome online community for IT Managed Service Providers (MSPs). When an MSP joins the Tech Tribe, Nigel uses a tool called Bonjoro to send a video message welcoming them to the Tribe.

Now, within the community are thousands of MSPs from all over the world, with hundreds more joining the Tribe every month – so, at the time of writing, Nigel has recorded well over 5000 video messages, with more being recorded every week.

Talk about remarkable!

If you feel uncomfortable about recording video, I want you to reflect on Nigel Moore's experience. Nigel tells me that when he first started recording these videos, he was nervous. He procrastinated, and then stumbled through his messages.

However, the feedback he received from Tribers was

overwhelmingly positive!

This encouraged Nigel to continue recording his video welcomes and, very quickly, he learned to be himself and simply talk to the camera as he'd talk to a person.

Practice makes perfect and, thousands of videos later, Nigel is well known for his warm personality in front of the camera as it shines through to MSPs all over the world.

> **Your Personal Brand**. We all know using the same fonts, colours, logo(s), styles and telling the same story across media and time builds your company's brand. We know everything we do, from issuing quotes to answering the phone, defines our brand. But how do we build our personal brand and become the interesting character that draws business to us?
>
> The first step is to define what makes you unique. This is analogous to defining your USP (unique selling proposition). It still thrills me to hear someone say, "You don't seem like an IT guy," and indeed, that is not my life. I've been a mechanic, worked in oil fields and on pipelines, played guitar, done journalism, and much more. I am not my job, and you are not yours.
>
> I always include a picture of myself (and our logo) in personal communications and posts. In our marketing I also try to include photos of our facility, staff and logo, prominently displayed. And we always try to 'sign' anything we do to identify it as our work, for example by leaving logo stickers on all equipment. This is great company branding – but let's get more personal yet.
>
> Joshua Liberman, Net Sciences

So, if you're nervous about recording a message, I'd encourage you to get started and use every excuse you can to send videos. Pretty soon, you'll find it as comfortable as typing out an email – except your video messages will be received a lot more positively than yet another email in your contacts' inbox!

I've mentioned Hippo Video and Bonjoro for their ability to quickly record videos directly from within your web browser and email client. Another similar tool is Vidyard, which is free to get started with.

Be the Connector - Again

We've already explored the concept of being a connector at a business networking event. But becoming a connector doesn't end at the event!

Yes, you can also be a connector *after* an event.

For instance, when I'm processing my business cards and new contacts, it encourages me to look for the opportunity to connect my new contact with somebody else within my network who I think they'll find valuable to meet.

For instance, if somebody says they want to improve their LinkedIn profile, I'll point them towards John Espirian, the relentlessly helpful LinkedIn nerd. And if my new contact has told me they are an IT business wanting to improve their marketing, I'll suggest they speak with marketing guru Paul Green.

I've even connected somebody who wanted chewing gum removed from a pavement with someone who specialises in removing chewing gum from pavements!

Remember, while you may never do business directly with the person you meet, you may be able to refer them to someone who does. In this way, you place yourself at the centre of a network of people – and don't be surprised when people try to reciprocate and return the favour.

The point here is that you are looking to add value to your new connections.

When you go to events, listen to people. Pay attention to what they do and what they say. Sadly, it's remarkable to be a listener nowadays – so you'll stand out from the crowd when you do.

Summary

In this chapter, we've looked at how business networking doesn't finish when the event ends.

- Schedule time to process business cards and follow up with your new contacts after an event.
- By creating memory hooks, you can follow up with people more effectively.
- Video messaging helps you stand out from the crowd.

- Remember that being the connector can add a lot of value to your new relationships.

If you follow these steps, you will be making sure the time you put into attending conferences, seminars and business networking events is well spent. It doesn't have to take much time or effort, but by having a repeatable system in place, you can deal with business cards quickly, grow your network effectively, and build relationships with the people who can help you make a difference.

> Taking a genuine interest in others will bring opportunities your way. In a kind of karmatic way, things seem to come back around.
>
> Tell people what you do clearly and with confidence and then spend your time learning, engaging and not hoping to sell something on the spot.
>
> You may never see that person again – or you could end up making a new acquaintance, a friend, a client or an advocate who turns into a master referrer.
>
> However it all works out, get out to meet people, have some fun and build your community – or, if you must, your network.
>
> Adam Foster, Starstream Data

Further Resources

- Article: *Thanks for your Friend Request – but do I know you?* https://tubb.co/whoareyou
- Resource: A list of Professional Service Automation tools for MSPs - https://tubb.co/psa
- Guide: How do I choose a CRM Vendor to work with? https://bit.ly/chooseacrm

- Hippo Video: https://www.hippovideo.io
- Vidyard Video Messaging for Business: https://tubb.co/vidyard
- Bonjoro Powerful Personal Videos: https://tubb.co/bonjoro

Making Business Introductions

We've already explored the opportunities you'll discover to be the connector as a result of business networking. Being a connector is an excellent way to add value to any of your business relationships because, by connecting two people, you'll make both parties feel respected and appreciated. Additionally, you will have created a potential business opportunity for somebody, while possibly helping someone else solve a business challenge. However, these introductions need to be made in the right way. You've got to be connecting people for the right reasons.

How to Make Good Business Introductions

If you are going to connect two people, firstly, make sure those two people want to be connected. I can't tell you the number of times I've received well-meaning yet ultimately frustrating unsolicited messages from business friends who have connected me with a contact, with little explanation as to why we were being connected.

Instead, a better way of connecting people is to ask both parties for permission to make the connection. For example, if somebody shares with you that they are facing a business challenge and your connector's antennae goes up with a sense you can introduce them to somebody who may be able to help, first ask them if this would be helpful!

Secondly, ask this person how important the introduction would be to them. It may be that they are not looking for help right now – in which case, tell them you'd be happy to make the introduction when the time is right for them. Leave the ball in their court.

Next, if the person agrees the introduction would be useful, and they'd like to speak to your contact, tell them you'll reach out to your contact to ask them if an introduction might be appropriate. After all, your contact might be extremely busy on a project or not taking on new work right now, which would create frustration for both parties if you were to press ahead and make an introduction anyway!

Finally, once you've got both parties' agreement for the introduction, go ahead and make the connection!

Here's an example of a typical business introduction email I use to connect two people, once I've sought their permission for the connection.

For the purposes of this example, Lara has mentioned to me she'd like some help with copywriting for her IT business, and Stephen is a friend of mine who is an excellent writer for technology businesses.

> Lara,
>
> As discussed, allow me to introduce my friend Stephen. Stephen is a friend and colleague of mine who runs Golden Writers Ltd, a company based out of Birmingham.
>
> The reason for the introduction is that you mentioned you were looking for some help with copywriting for your website, and Stephen is one of the best writers I know! I'd definitely recommend speaking to Stephen to see if he can help your business.
>
> @Stephen – Lara is my friend from Cape Town and she runs a technology business. Based on what Lara has told me about her requirements, I think you may be a great fit.
>
> @Both – I'll step out at this stage and leave you two to connect directly, if appropriate.
>
> Richard

As you can tell, in this introduction email I've done a number of things:

- I've connected Lara and Stephen, with their mutual permission.
- I have given a quick overview of who each party is, and a reminder of why I'm connecting them.
- I've given permission for the two contacts to continue the conversation *without me being involved* (to avoid my inbox being clogged up!).

In my experience, the above format works really well – and I believe I've connected a lot of very good people together.

The bottom line here is that I've respected everyone's time and boundaries by seeking their permission to make an introduction. However, if you don't respect everyone's time then the introduction can go wrong, and this can lead to frustration all round.

> Networking in your local area isn't just about 'networking' and passing a business card, it's about getting to know people: who they are, what they do, what problems they are experiencing – and I'm not just talking about tech.
>
> After all, we all experience problems and having someone to talk to about them can be a real help.
>
> When you show genuine interest in someone and create a human connection, you close the gap between being unknown and known.
>
> Ask yourself this: who do you turn to when you have a problem? Is it someone unknown or is it someone you have met, believe you can trust, and believe will get the job done?
>
> Adam Foster, Starstream Data

An Example of a Business Introduction Gone Wrong

To give you an insight into a less than successful introduction, let me share a story about a friend of mine who made a warm connection to someone she thought I should get to know.

This person had told my friend they were looking for somebody to help them with a challenge within their IT business. Being a connector, my friend naturally thought of me and suggested to the business owner that I might be able to help. The business owner agreed and asked my friend to make an introduction.

So, my friend introduced me to this person via an email and in glowing terms. The email went on to give a summary of why my friend felt it would be of benefit to us both to connect.

The first lesson here is that when you're making an introduction between two people, by being the connector you are acting as an advocate for both parties. Implicitly, you're recommending these people to one another. Therefore, you want to make sure the two parties being connected are people you can vouch for and trust.

Back to our introduction story… Grateful to my friend for thinking of me in this way, I promptly responded to the email and shared a bit about myself and my background. The next day, the business owner responded to my email, courteous in his response, but simply offering a one-line thanks for the introduction, with no request to continue the conversation.

My friend clearly felt a bit awkward after reading this reply and apologised to me for the brief email I'd received. I reassured my friend and suggested to her that perhaps the other party was busy and would be in touch properly when he had a chance.

But we both knew the repercussions of this contact's response. The introduction clearly wasn't important to the business owner, who was probably working long hours with lots of urgent tasks on his plate. While he probably felt a courteous short reply would move this 'additional work' off his plate, the reality is that he signalled to both my friend and me that we weren't important to him. Or at least, not important to him at that moment.

Clearly, the business owner did need help, but rather than setting the expectations of my friend and asking her to make the introduction at a later date, they didn't truly respect my friend's time – nor mine. Even after the introduction had been made, they could have thanked my friend for the connection and then set my expectations that they would like to connect now for a discussion at a later date. Instead, they effectively ended the conversation.

The result? My friend would now think twice before making any further introductions to this individual.

Interestingly, this person reached out to me almost a year later to connect, but I must admit that I was wary of engaging because of the way he had behaved in the past. Our relationship won't develop and, in turn, I won't make any introductions to him, which also could have been of value to his business.

The lesson here is to treat new business connections with respect – both for the person you're being connected with, and the person who connected you.

Or, to put it another way, a new business connection is an opportunity to make two people feel valued for their effort.

How You Should Deal with Introductions Made to You

So how do I think the business owner should have dealt with the introduction?

Well, he might have:

- Thanked our mutual friend profusely for thinking of him

and taking the time to make the introduction.

- Warmly greeted me and checked out my website, to demonstrate a bit of understanding of who I was and how I might be able to help him.
- Set my expectations that he would connect with me directly so his friend isn't copied into the rest of our emails, cluttering her inbox.
- Set my expectations of a time he'd like to continue the conversation (either now or in the future) or offer some times that he'd like to chat further.

Perhaps the business owner and I had something in common. Perhaps not. But if his friend took the time to make the introduction, we should take the time to respect that generosity by exploring it further.

More often than not, we place too much priority on emails; they distract us from the important work we should be doing. But despite the overwhelm of too many emails, we should appreciate the importance of some of them.

Our response (or lack of response) to those emails may influence how others view us now and in the future. This leads us to think about why relationships are important, and why we should take time to nurture them.

Summary

In this chapter, we've explored how to make and receive good business networking introductions.

- Before connecting two people, first seek out the permission of the people involved.

- Ask both parties whether the introduction is convenient now or should be made at a later date.

- During the email introduction, give both parties a brief introduction to the other, and then remind them why you're introducing them.

- After making an introduction step out of the conversation, so your inbox isn't clogged up.

- Respect any new connections that are shared with you, as these introductions have powerful implications for your relationship with both the introducer and the new contact.

Now we've covered in-person networking, it's time to move on to the often thorny subject of social or online networking. Many business owners are suspicious of social media, concerned about the blurring of personal and professional lives, or just don't know where to begin.

Hopefully, this next section will help you have a better understanding of what social networking (or online networking) is and how it can benefit your business and strengthen relationships with your connections.

Why You Should Use Social Networking for Business (If You Don't Already)

Nowadays, it seems as though everyone is online. Platforms such as Facebook, Twitter, LinkedIn, Instagram, Pinterest, YouTube, TikTok and others have become a ubiquitous part of our lives.

Whether you call it social media, social networking or online networking, one question always crops up in my conversations with IT professionals: "Is this stuff actually valuable for me to use in business?"

My answer to this question is yes, absolutely! Social networking should form a big part of your business networking strategy. However, many business people don't understand social networking and its benefits, and they either ignore it or, worse, embrace it and it ends up becoming a time sink.

There is also a tendency to think that social networking is a replacement for more traditional forms of networking and that you no longer need to meet people at business networking events. In reality, I'd suggest that social networking and in-person business networking work hand in hand.

How Engagement on Social Networks Differs from In-person Networking

In-person business networking is limited by the amount of time you can spend out in the world.

Social networking allows you to maintain a lot of relationships from behind your keyboard.

I consider myself a person to whom relationships are very

important, so I spend a lot of time meeting people and keeping in touch with others via the telephone. However, I know I'm not alone when I think of somebody I know, or a person's name comes up in conversation, and I say, "I've been meaning to catch up with them."

Social networking allows you to keep in touch with people more effectively. You can use it to let your more active connections know what you're up to, add value to conversations, share information of mutual interest, and much more.

Even if someone you know doesn't use social networking much, you can keep in touch with them quickly and easily via email – send a link with a note saying: "I thought you might be interested in this article I wrote/found/had passed on to me."

> Social media helps us create hype around the topic and the speakers, extending our reach to their network. If you want to be an authority in your field this will help immensely.
>
> Over time you can build a strong mailing list, which also makes a difference when organising an event.
>
> Just ensure it's well segmented: if you have a specific target in mind for your event, don't 'over invite'. It's better to have a smaller, targeted audience than a scatter approach.
>
> Vera Tucci, T-Consulting

The thing is, these methods are not time-consuming, yet they are very powerful for maintaining a relationship between phone calls or meetings.

It works in reverse, too. If you spend all your time doing social networking, just like spending all your time doing traditional networking you'll get some results, but you're missing an opportunity to take things further.

You'll quickly find, like I have, that you can build a relationship with someone who's found you online (or you found them) through social networking, and then you can take it to the next level by organising a meet up at a face-to-face event.

Social networking is really no different to traditional networking – the aims and outcomes are the same. But each individual has their own preference for communicating, so it makes sense to have the right tools to stay in touch with them.

If you're still not convinced, you may be interested to know that, contrary to popular belief, there are some personal benefits to social networking, too.

Let's dive in by first understanding why you should be using social networking to effectively complement your in-person business networking.

> I do not believe that social media on its own is valuable for networking and relationships. I believe in the mantra 'people buy people' and that means they're not buying a service, they're buying the person who represents that service. If you've never met someone, or never talked, and only interacted over social media, how will someone feel comfortable giving you high-value opportunities? It may seem old skool now, but meeting people, talking to people, finding out what they need and opportunities that would work for them is the only way to go in my opinion.
>
> Craig Sharp, Abussi

Find Support via Social Networking

Running an IT business can be a lonely, thankless task. You will have client support tickets to deal with, quotes and proposals to create, plus you need to be marketing yourself to stay front of mind.

All these tasks remind me that there were times when I wondered why I'd even chosen to be an IT professional! I started to consider whether I should chuck it all in and go open a fishing tackle store (and I've never even been fishing!).

I want to demonstrate why social networking can help you build even stronger relationships and find the support you need to keep going.

A frequent complaint (typically coming from those people who take a dim view of technology) is that the internet and social networking are contributing to the crumbling of traditional communities. We're told that instead of spending time meeting and talking with real people face-to-face, more people are instead tapping away at their keyboards.

This might be partly true, but I'm sure I'm not alone in thanking sites such as Facebook, Twitter and LinkedIn for helping me connect with new business contacts and friends. Additionally, social networking has reconnected me with friends and people from the past with whom I've lost touch and, indeed, helped to deepen relationships with existing contacts from many different areas of my life.

We've all bumped into someone we've lost contact with by chance and had those conversations where one person says: "We should stay in touch!" But how often does it actually happen? Much as we'd like to make those regular phone calls or visits, busy lives and other circumstances often prevent that from happening.

One of the upsides of social networking is that it makes it easier to passively keep in touch with groups of friends, colleagues or business contacts and update them on what's happening in your life – and vice versa. Often, spotting an update from a contact I've been meaning to call results in me picking up the phone and ringing them with a specific subject in mind – their latest status update.

Remember the social aspect of social networking, and never forget that there is a real person on the other end of your keyboard.

Connect with People on a Human Level

Just before I sold my IT business, my father, George, passed away. Dad had reached the ripe old age at 82, but naturally his death came as a shock. And I found, like many others who've experienced such a bereavement, that I suddenly had responsibilities.

For instance, my family and I needed to contact close friends and relatives to break the bad news. We also needed to organise a funeral, sort out paperwork, and do all this while managing our emotions at Dad's passing.

Once we'd told those closest to us about Dad's death, Mom and I agreed to share the news with our friends on Facebook. The support we received from friends and neighbours who'd found our news online was incredible. We received some truly wonderful and kind messages of support from many different people – all of which made a difficult time a whole lot easier.

We also realised that people wanted to know how they could pay their respects and be notified of the funeral arrangements. Rather than having flowers (as Dad was never keen on them), we asked people to make donations to his favourite charity, and we were able to set up a site in Dad's memory.

We shared the funeral details on social networks as well as in the newspaper and we were touched by the large turnout. Being connected to so many friends and family in this way helped us all during a very difficult time.

Hopefully, as you get more comfortable with social networking, you'll be able to share meaningful, significant events in your life too. Whether happy or sad, reaching out to people in a large-scale way can bring unexpected results -- both personally and professionally.

We don't live in a world where we have enough time to keep in touch with everyone who matters to us, but I think social networking is a positive contributor in the modern world. It doesn't replace offline activities, but it does help to keep us connected.

And whatever you do, try to remember that whether you're using LinkedIn, Facebook, Twitter or another social networking platform, it is human nature for us to show the best sides of ourselves – and not the whole story.

> Confidence grows from doing the do and taking off the pressure of perfect.
>
> Each and every time you network, chunk down your approach to a slice and a sprout or two and have a go.
>
> You never know, you might even find you grow to enjoy the process!
>
> Dave Algeo, Networking Wingman and Restless Midlifer

Boost Your Confidence

How many times have you browsed through your Facebook feed and wondered why everyone else is having wonderful adventures, amazing experiences and generally living their best lives, while you're stuck at home feeling miserable?

Or perhaps you've scrolled through the LinkedIn news feed and wondered why everyone you know seems to be successful in business, when you feel as though you're struggling to grow your own company or career?

In fact, the impression you will often get from others' social networking profiles is simply their life's highlight reel.

Let me explain by using myself as an example. If you follow me on Twitter at twitter.com/tubblog then you'll know I tweet about the IT industry. By following my tweets, you'll also quickly realise that I enjoy playing with a lot of cool geeky gadgets. Oh, and I enjoy eating lovely food at great restaurants.

Plus, if you follow me on Instagram, or we're close enough to be friends on my personal Facebook account, then you'll know I'm always having a roaring good time with my vast circle of close friends, who, incidentally, are fabulous.

Yes, I travel the world, visiting fantastic places, eating good food, and hob-nobbing with some of the most intelligent, beautiful and amazing people!

Right?

Well, there's some truth in there but I rarely post a social networking update sharing the boring things I do every day. Grinding out work, doing housework or going shopping. Nor, in fact, do I often share on social networking the challenges I'm facing. It's not often I share how I'm feeling awfully low during a bout of clinical depression, or how I'm in bed feeling like crap with the flu.

In fact, most of us only post the cool and exciting to our social networking accounts, and that's understandable. Why would we post the boring or the mundane? That's not what we want to be noticed for.

I'm like most people. If I travel somewhere cool – I'll share it. If I'm enjoying a good time with great friends – I'll share it.

That recent Friday night when I sat at home feeling utterly miserable, attractively stuffing my face with pizza and ice cream? Not shared so much!

And this will be true of the people you interact and connect with too. Yet despite this, we all find ourselves comparing our normal lives to the highlight reels we see on social networking profiles.

Let's put a stop to this. It's an unfair comparison.

An old friend once helped me put it into perspective when she said: "Sometimes, when I see all the cool stuff you're doing on Facebook, I laugh, because it's you!"

Essentially, what she meant was my Facebook feed (my highlight reel) didn't reflect my true life, with all its lumps and bumps, ups and downs, to someone who knows me well.

Pastor Steven Furtick once said: "One reason we struggle with insecurity is that we're comparing our behind-the-scenes to everyone else's highlight reel."

Comparing your own all-encompassing view of your life with the highlight reel of someone else's life can create insecurities. It can also create resentment. It shouldn't, but it's human nature.

It's a lot like going to a party. You scrub up. You wear your nicest clothes that make you look your best. During small talk with others, you share the cool things that are happening in your life. You accentuate all the good bits about you – and understandably so. It's the stuff you're proud of and want to share.

But the reality may be different. Few amongst us want to highlight the stuff we've failed at, or the mistakes we've made, or the disappointments we've experienced.

It's worth remembering that.

So, the next time you are feeling a little low, and become irritated by another super-cool picture or super-positive update from a Facebook friend or LinkedIn business contact, just remember that you're seeing their highlight reel.

There is absolutely, positively (no two ways around it) also stuff happening behind the scenes to that person that more than likely mirrors the struggles everyone else has or will experience.

In short, comparing your normal life to the highlights you glean of others' lives on social networking sites is an inaccurate comparison.

Social networking can promote negative feelings, if not managed properly. Instead, make sure you use the platforms mindfully. Used well, social networking should help you feel more connected and boost your confidence, not undermine it.

Give Kudos to Others and Respond to Comments

Have you ever left a comment for a business or brand online, and not got a response? Perhaps you've tweeted a company to give them feedback on something they've done wrong. You posted your tweet and then... crickets. They don't respond. Or, at best, they respond weeks afterwards, leaving you puzzling as to what your original message was about.

It's not a nice feeling to feel like you're being ignored, so I want to encourage you to take on a new mantra for your online activities.

No Comment Left Behind.

If somebody takes the time to leave a comment on one of your social networking posts, I want you to respect them enough to take the time to respond. Your response could be as simple as: "Thank you for taking the time to respond."

If somebody takes the time to share your article, thank them for sharing the article with their own community.

Unless you are Bill Gates, who has 61.1 million Twitter followers (at the time of writing), and so can be forgiven for not responding to the thousands of messages he receives every day, you're unlikely to be swamped with messages. And every one of those messages is sent by a human being, who appreciates being seen and acknowledged.

Remember that social networking is a conversation, not a platform for you to shout from. Just like in real life, if somebody starts a conversation with you, it's polite to respond.

Make sure no comment is left behind.

Summary

In this chapter, we've explored why you should be using social networking and the benefits it brings to your business relationships.

- Social networking and in-person networking complement each other effectively.
- Social networking allows you to passively maintain relationships with larger groups of people.
- You can find valuable personal and professional support via

social networking channels.

- Be aware of the dangers of social networking – don't fall into the trap of comparing your backstage to others' highlights.

- No comment left behind. Respond to all comments you receive online.

In the next chapter, we'll explore some tactics for using LinkedIn, the biggest business-focused social networking channel in the world.

Business Networking on LinkedIn

When it comes to online business networking, there is one clear leader: LinkedIn. While Twitter and Facebook are popular for business, LinkedIn, with 875 million members from 200 countries and regions worldwide, allows you to build your online presence on the world's biggest professional networking platform. It's where a lot of decision-makers congregate, and it's the platform where you can be found by your next ideal client or business partner, completely for free!

It's also a great tool to use before, during and after your attendance at networking events to support and accelerate your business networking.

Before An Event: Sort Out Your LinkedIn Profile

When you meet people at an in-person business networking event, they get to meet the real you. They get to see you and hear you talk about yourself and your business. And after you've met someone at an event, the two places people are most likely to go to in order to find out more about you are your website and, you've guessed it, LinkedIn!

It's also worth remembering that in the modern age of business networking, there are likely to be dozens, if not hundreds (or thousands!) of people you will do business with that you may **never meet in person!**

Therefore, for people who have already met you in person, and for those who have never met you at all, it's important that your LinkedIn profile is a good representation of who you are, what you do and what you stand for.

So, how can you tailor your LinkedIn profile to be effective for your business networking efforts?

I've asked John Espirian, author of the book *Content DNA* (https://espirian.co.uk/book/) and host of the LinkedIn-focused Espresso+ community (https://espirian.co.uk/join/) for his wisdom on how IT professionals can effectively use LinkedIn.

Update Your LinkedIn Profile

The core of your LinkedIn presence is found in your LinkedIn profile, which comprises dozens of fields. Just as with the advice for making a good website, the most important part of your LinkedIn profile is at the very top.

Why? Because readers are lazy: if you don't capture their attention before they start scrolling, the chances of them seeing something interesting further down the profile is very low.

That said, it doesn't mean the rest of your profile doesn't matter. Lots of fields inside LinkedIn are searchable, and if you have just the right skill or experience that someone is looking for then your profile may be shown in search results anyway.

The so-called 'top card' of your LinkedIn profile is where you will catch people's attention. This contains a few key pieces of information that give context to what your profile is all about. Whether you're a service provider or you sell a product, this is the place to plant your flag and convey your value proposition with a short, clear, differentiated hook.

Let's take a look at some of the features in the top card of the LinkedIn profile.

Use a Strong Profile Picture

Along with your name, your profile photo will follow you all around LinkedIn. Don't underestimate the value of a well-framed, well-lit photo. We are tuned to respond positively to welcoming faces, so present an engaging look to your prospective viewer, and you should get more people clicking through to find out more about you.

Your background banner image sits at the very top of your profile and is prime visual real estate for conveying your value proposition. Use an image that has 4:1 dimensions (that's four times as wide as tall).

Free tools such as Canva can help you create a banner. This may be sufficient for getting started, though ultimately you might want to use a design professional to give your profile a polished look.

Note that your profile photo will be partially overlaid on the banner image. This means it's not smart to put anything of strategic importance in the bottom-left corner of the banner, else you risk it being obscured by your photo.

LinkedIn said in 2022 that 70% of all LinkedIn traffic comes via the LinkedIn mobile app*, so you should think 'mobile first' when optimising your profile. In the case of the banner image, that means keeping the visuals and text large and clear. (*Source: https://youtube.com/watch?v=c1hOnApqOgU&t=1580s)

Optimise Your Profile

Your profile headline can be up to 220 characters in length but note that a headline that uses all those characters would look like a wall of text on a mobile. Less is more. I recommend optimising the first 40 characters of the headline to convey the value proposition in an interesting, differentiated manner. This headline opening is particularly important because it is the only text that many mobile users will see when they look at your posts and comments.

Create a Profile Video

My best tip for humanising the top card of your LinkedIn profile is to record a 30-second profile video. This is a portrait-mode video that you can upload only via the LinkedIn mobile app. People who view your profile can see that video by clicking on your profile photo.

I find this immensely powerful when assessing a profile: if someone makes a good impression in that profile video, that's sufficient for me to want to know more about them. Conversely, a bad or missing profile video is a missed opportunity to turn a viewer into a potential customer.

Create an Audio Pronunciation

The little brother of the profile video is the audio pronunciation field. Again, this is

something that can be added only via the LinkedIn mobile app. You get 10 seconds to record how your name ought to be pronounced, and you can also use that time to show a bit of personality and invite people to get in touch.

During the Event: Use the LinkedIn App

In a later chapter, we're going to explore how to deal effectively with the business cards you collect during an in-person business event. However, it's worth mentioning that increasingly, exchanging business cards is falling out of favour as the best way to exchange contact information.

Instead, tools such as the LinkedIn mobile app allow people to connect with one another in the moment using their smartphones.

The Find Nearby Feature

If you download the LinkedIn app (iOS, Android) and enable Bluetooth sharing, you can use Find Nearby to discover other LinkedIn members around you (up to 100 feet / 30 metres). This feature is handy if you're attending an event and want to see who is in the room (or, like me, you struggle to connect names with faces).

In order to use the Find Nearby feature, you will first need to activate Bluetooth on your mobile device. Next, within the LinkedIn mobile app, tap the My Network tab and tap the blue circle button. Finally, in the pop-up menu, tap the Find Nearby icon to see all nearby LinkedIn members.

If a nearby member is already a LinkedIn connection, you'll see the option to send them a message. If not, you can invite them to connect.

When Find Nearby is switched on, other LinkedIn members can discover you, even when you're not using the LinkedIn mobile app. You can check or change your Find Nearby status on the My Network tab by following this same process.

LinkedIn QR Codes

Another way you can use the LinkedIn mobile app is through using QR codes. For instance, say you meet someone at an event and want to quickly connect with them via LinkedIn, you can find and share your unique QR code with them.

To find your QR code, open the LinkedIn mobile app and tap the QR code icon at the right end of the search bar.

When the LinkedIn code screen opens, you'll see two tabs: Scan and My Code. Open the My Code tab to find your QR code for sharing.

On the Scan tab, you scan in someone else's code and go straight to their LinkedIn profile.

Simple!

> Pro Tip: I've saved my LinkedIn QR code as an image and then set it as a custom lock screen on my smartphone. Then, when I'm at in-person events, it's much quicker to whip my phone out and show someone my QR code than to unlock and open the LinkedIn app each time I want to connect with the person. Thanks, John Espirian, for the tip!

After The Event: Follow Up on LinkedIn

In an earlier chapter, we explored the idea that business networking doesn't end when you leave a networking event. In fact, the most important part of networking might be the follow-up! And LinkedIn has a huge part to play in your follow-up efforts.

Customise Your LinkedIn Connection Request

First, to make sure you're connecting effectively with people on

LinkedIn I recommend customising your connection requests and avoiding what I refer to as the 'boiler plate' method.

What is the boiler plate method, and why do I loathe it so much?

Well, we all know the standard message LinkedIn defaults to when you go to add a new connection. In my opinion, this boilerplate "I'd like to add you to my professional network on LinkedIn" is lazy and, frankly, it sucks.

For example, what's in it for the other person to connect with you? Why do you want to connect? Remind me, who even are you?

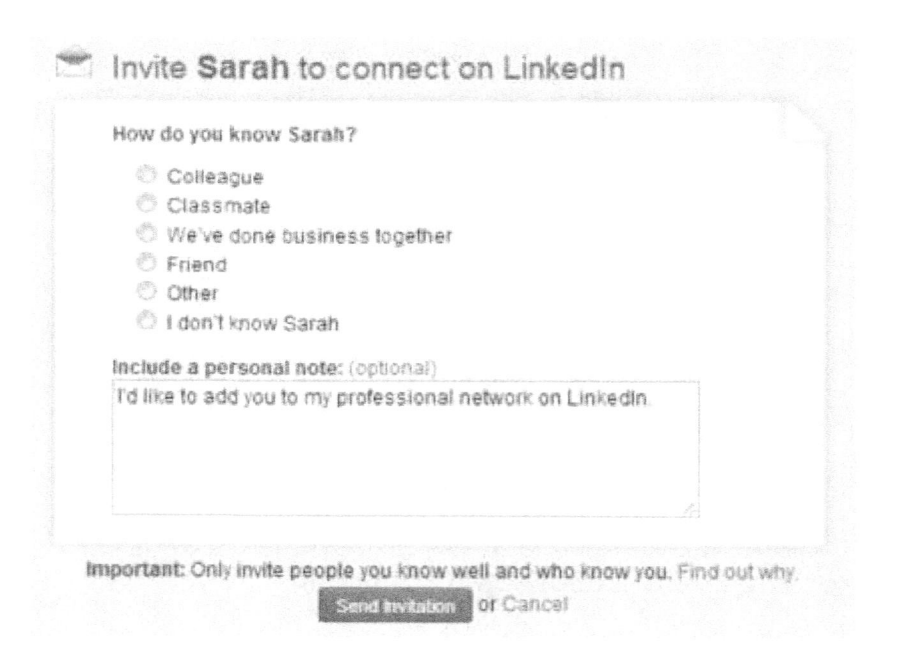

> **Invite Sarah to connect on LinkedIn**
>
> How do you know Sarah?
> - Colleague
> - Classmate
> - We've done business together
> - Friend
> - Other
> - I don't know Sarah
>
> Include a personal note: (optional)
>
> I'd like to add you to my professional network on LinkedIn.
>
> Important: Only invite people you know well and who know you. Find out why.
>
> **Send Invitation** or Cancel

So, I recommend avoiding using the standard "Let's connect on LinkedIn" as it appears spam-like in nature, and instead sending a bespoke connection message. Customise this message to remind the person of where you met and give them a compelling reason to connect with you.

For example, your message might be as simple as:

Hi David, it was great to meet you at the business breakfast earlier today! I really enjoyed our conversation about sustainable methods for growing a business. I thought it might be useful for us to connect on LinkedIn to help stay in touch?

Similar to the method we used earlier for an effective email follow-up, in this LinkedIn connection request we've:

- Reminded the person where we met
- Given the person a memory hook of what we talked about
- Suggested to the person why it is a good idea we connect on LinkedIn

This method is simple, yet effective. It helps you stand out from a sea of boring boilerplate "Let's connect on LinkedIn" messages.

Send a LinkedIn Video Message

In an earlier chapter, we talked about the power of using video to stand out from the crowd in your follow-up messages. Well, networking via LinkedIn is no exception! You can record a video message for your LinkedIn recipients directly from within the LinkedIn mobile app on iOS and Android platforms. But, once again, just because this tool is available doesn't mean everybody is actively using it!

Think back to the last time you received a video message on LinkedIn. How did you react? I bet it made you smile and take notice.

Or perhaps you've *never* received a LinkedIn video message!

In either case, if you start using video messages within LinkedIn, you can expect to stand out from the crowd and get some very positive feedback.

Make no mistake, video as a form of communication is remarkable – and it is here to stay. Therefore, I'd encourage you to make sure you embrace video within your business networking.

Summary

In this chapter, we've explored why LinkedIn is the world's most popular business social networking site and how you can effectively use LinkedIn to strengthen your business relationships and put yourself out there.

- Focus on developing the 'top card' of your LinkedIn profile.
- Use a well-framed, well-lit profile picture.
- Create a compelling 4:1 banner image.
- Optimise your profile headline.
- Consider how your profile will look on mobile devices.
- Setup a 30-second profile video and audio pronunciation field.
- When connecting with new contacts, customise your message and avoid using the 'boiler plate' standard default
- Use the LinkedIn mobile app to send a video message to help you stand out from the crowd.

In our next chapter, we're going to look at some simple tactics to enable you to use Twitter more effectively as part of your social networking strategy.

Further Resources

- The LinkedIn Leaders Playbook (https://espirian.co.uk/linkedin-course/).

- Book: *Content DNA* by John Espirian (https://espirian.co.uk/book/).
- Ongoing learning, support and accountability for business owners who want to build an effective presence on LinkedIn and online: The Espresso+ community (https://espirian.co.uk/join/).

Business Networking on Twitter

When talking about social networking, we've mostly been focused on using LinkedIn. But LinkedIn isn't the only social networking platform for business owners.

My personal favourite platform is Twitter – or 'X', as it has been rebranded after Elon Musk's takeover. For the purposes of this book, I'm going to refer to X as Twitter, because, well, I don't know anyone else who calls it X. Sorry, Elon.

The three reasons I like Twitter are:

1. Twitter allows me to quickly and easily share with people what I'm doing, where I'm going and who I'm spending time with. (As we explored in an earlier chapter, this is an important part of business networking.)

2. I can engage in asynchronous conversations with a large number of people (or Tweeps!) about topics I'm passionate about, including my business.

3. Twitter gives me the opportunity to share my content -- such as blog posts, articles, podcasts and videos -- with a wide audience.

Now, I'm an author, speaker and content creator, so I've got plenty to share! However, Twitter can be a powerful platform for you as an IT business, too.

Use Twitter to Connect with Your Peers

Firstly, Twitter is a great platform for connecting with your peers – other technology businesses. As we'll explore in depth in a later chapter, business networking isn't just about meeting potential clients, it is also about building strong strategic relationships that can help your business grow.

On Twitter, you can search for relevant hashtags like #ManagedServices, follow influencers and thought leaders, and engage in conversations with other MSPs. This can lead to valuable networking opportunities, such as partnerships or referrals.

Use Twitter to Stay Informed

Secondly, Twitter can help you stay up to date with industry news and trends. By following key accounts and monitoring relevant hashtags, you can keep abreast of the latest developments in the world of IT and MSPs. This can help you stay competitive and ensure that your business is always at the forefront of our industry.

Use Twitter to Connect with Prospective Clients

Thirdly, Twitter can be a great platform for promoting your business and showcasing your expertise. By tweeting about your services, sharing blog posts or articles, and engaging with potential clients, you can build your brand and attract new customers. Plus, by demonstrating your knowledge and expertise on Twitter, you can establish yourself as a thought leader in the industry.

Overall, there are plenty of reasons why MSP owners should be using Twitter for business networking activities. But how can you use Twitter effectively, and not get pulled into the time sink of Twitter's Matrix-like stream of consciousness?

Use Twitter Lists

If you're already using Twitter, this next tip may help you take your experience to the next level! Check out Twitter lists – they can be a total game-changer!

Twitter lists can help you stay organised. If you're following a lot of different accounts, it can be hard to keep track of everything. By creating lists of accounts that are related to specific topics or interests, you can keep your Twitter feed more manageable and make sure you're not missing out on anything important.

For instance, you might want to create Twitter lists such as:

- Local businesses – potential clients who you'd like to engage with

- Existing clients – to ensure you can effectively follow their news and maintain your relationship

- Journalists – who may be looking for your help with a story

- Strategic partners – businesses who you could work with to deliver solutions to your clients

- Influencers – industry thought leaders who you want to learn from

Twitter lists can help you build relationships with other users more effectively. By creating lists of accounts that are relevant to you, you can engage with those users more easily and foster connections. You can retweet their content, reply to their tweets, and generally show that you're paying attention to what they're saying. This can help you build your own following and establish yourself as an authority in your field.

As you can see, while the maelstrom of information that is Twitter can lead to information overload, Twitter lists help you spend your time on the platform more efficiently. Plus, Twitter lists can help you discover new accounts to follow. By browsing other users' public lists or searching for lists related to your interests, you can find new accounts that you might not otherwise have discovered.

This can help you broaden your network and find new sources of inspiration.

For example, check out my own curated Twitter list of MSP IT vendors (https://twitter.com/i/lists/47786892) or tech journalists (https://twitter.com/i/lists/64650299).

Overall, Twitter lists can be a powerful tool for any Twitter user. Whether you're using them to stay organised, discover new accounts or build relationships, they're definitely worth checking out. So why not give them a try and see how they can benefit you?

Summary

In this chapter, we've explored why Twitter can be a powerful tool for business networking, and how you can use Twitter lists to become a Twitter power user.

- Twitter is a great platform for connecting with your peers – other technology businesses – with whom you can build strategic alliances.

- Twitter can help you stay up to date with industry news and trends. To do so, follow key accounts and relevant hashtags.

- Twitter can be a great platform for promoting your business and showcasing your expertise. By demonstrating your knowledge and expertise on Twitter, you can establish yourself as a thought leader in your space.

- You can set up Twitter lists to stay organised and keep your Twitter feed more manageable.

We've looked at how you can use social networking to connect and chat with people online. In the next chapter we'll look at another power of social networking – the ability to listen to your clients.

Using Social Networking to Listen to Customer Feedback

Up until this point in this book, we've explored using social networking as a way to further develop relationships with new contacts. However, social networking channels are also a means to enable you to listen to customer feedback. What do people say about your business when they don't realise you're listening?

Hopefully, they say very nice things – but when it comes to social networking, human nature tends to lend itself towards people venting their frustrations. As a result, you might consider that monitoring social networking gives you a good chance to engage with existing clients you are in danger of losing, as well as keeping an ear out for potential new relationships with those people who are looking to work with somebody else.

For example, I once picked up a new MSP client by responding to a tweet where a business owner expressed his exasperation with his printer not working. By offering my support and solving the issue, I won this business owner's trust. Some time later, that business chose to move their custom to my MSP.

Monitoring Twitter

The interactions businesses have with customers can vary, depending on the comments made. For example, if someone tweets "Looking forward to staying at the Red Lion Hotel in Devon," the hotel owner could make sure they had a complimentary bottle of wine waiting upon arrival, with a note thanking them for the tweet.

It can also be used to help resolve complaints. Perhaps an

individual at the restaurant said that everything about their meal was to their satisfaction, but then tweeted "Had meal at The Hen and Chickens tonight. Was nice, but the gravy was cold." The opportunity here is obvious.

Remember that your clients may not feel comfortable sharing their frustrations with you directly, but they may take to social networking to express their exasperation. Therefore, it's worth using tools to keep track of mentions of your business online.

For example, some hotels and restaurants actively search social networking and media channels for people mentioning their brand name, so they can engage with those people directly.

Here's a personal example of how I found this out!

Story: The Metropole Hotel

I once stayed at the Metropole Hotel in Llandrindod Wells, Wales, where I was speaking at an IT conference at the venue. Being an environmentally conscious sort of chap, I'd really liked that the hotel had installed some green power-saving features in my hotel room and felt compelled to share this on social networking (with the hope that other hotels would be inspired to follow this green lead!). However, later on, I also took to Twitter to lament the fact that I was disappointed by the shower in my bathroom not working.

I gave this no more thought until after checkout, when I received an email from the hotel's managing director. To my pleasant surprise, the Metropole's MD thanked me for the feedback, said he'd checked the room I'd stayed in and explained that a 'non-return valve' in the shower had broken, but it was now fixed, and he offered the hotel's apologies.

Impressed, I naturally updated my Twitter feed to compliment the hotel on its dedication to customer service.

What just happened?

- As a customer, I liked the fact that somebody was listening to my feedback.

- More importantly, I felt **acknowledged** by the managing director's response. How many times have you complained about something only for it to be shrugged off, or for your complaint to be heard only for you to walk away saying: "They'll not bother to do anything about that."

- Other people, who I've never met and never will meet, may eyeball my tweets about the Metropole (or this chapter) and decide they want to stay at a venue like that – creating favourable potential customers.

Essentially, the experience I've described here meant my opinion of this hotel went from being a passive customer to an active fan. The staff at the Metropole are clearly doing a good job of engaging with existing and potential customers!

Wouldn't you like more raving fans of your business to tell others how great you are to work with?

Social Networking Monitoring Tools

No chapter on social networking for geeks would be complete without listing some shiny tools for you to try out!

The first tool I'd recommend you look at is Google Alerts (https://www.google.com/alerts), which allows you to monitor the web for interesting new content. Specifically in our case, we can use Google Alerts to monitor the web for keywords such as:

- Your business name
- Your website
- The names of your team members

Every time Google comes across new content, it will send you an email with a link to where you've been mentioned.

I've found Google Alerts to be a very useful tool for monitoring the web for mentions of my brand – and the best part? It's absolutely free to use!

Another tool I've used for monitoring social networking is Awario (https://awario.com/). It's a brand monitoring tool that allows you to monitor social networks for mentions of your brand **and the sentiment behind these mentions**.

Unlike Google Alerts, Awario is a paid tool, but in my experience it goes much deeper into the web than Google Alerts, finding all sorts of interesting mentions of your brand that you may otherwise have missed.

Summary

They say your brand is what people say about you when you're not in the room. And social networking gives anyone the opportunity to talk about your brand.

If you want to know what people are saying about your brand, and respond accordingly, you need to be listening and making it easy for people to contact you. For instance, do you have a Facebook business page so people can tell others how much they love you? What about a Twitter profile, or a LinkedIn page? If you're not visible on these platforms, you can't get involved in the conversation.

Additionally, you can use social networking monitoring to keep an eye out for conversations where you can add value. For example, if you're an MSP in Banbury, a regular search on "IT Support Banbury" could yield a number of opportunities to engage with companies or individuals who are looking for a chat about the subject.

I encourage you to try it and see!

So far in this book we've looked at business networking in-person and using social networking for business. In the next chapter, we'll look at the hybrid child of business networking and social networking – the virtual event.

Business Networking at Virtual Events

Does anyone remember March 2020? It was the month when the majority of the world went into lockdown as a result of the global COVID-19 pandemic.

I also remember March 2020 as 'The Great Working from Home Stampede', when IT professionals everywhere became essential workers for the world of business, as everyone asked their IT support providers to enable them to work remotely.

Fast-forward to the present day: the world of technology has been changed immeasurably by COVID-19, and those changes have extended to the world of business networking, too.

As a result of the inability to mix in-person during the pandemic, we saw the rise of the virtual event. We had virtual networking, virtual conferences, virtual peer groups, virtual user groups... If it could be done virtually, it was.

And for many people, this was no bad thing at all. If you found in-person networking events challenging, doing them from behind a keyboard and webcam was maybe more comfortable.

Whatever the case, nowadays you can find as many virtual business networking opportunities as you can find in-person events.

Attending virtual business events has its benefits, including cost-effectiveness, flexibility and accessibility. However, attending these events requires a slightly different approach than physical events.

Unfortunately, some people don't seem to attend virtual events with the same degree of professionalism as they do for in-person events.

Behaving Badly at Virtual Events

"You're right, it was bad. It should have been a lot better."

Not the words Pascal Fintoni was at all expecting to hear from his client after he had been critical of their last virtual conference.

Pascal is a friend and mentor of mine, and one of Europe's top speakers on digital marketing.

The event Pascal hosted was virtual, and Pascal's role was to emcee the event – introducing the various speakers, facilitating the question-and-answer sessions and delivering the closing keynote.

The day after the event, Pascal was invited to a post-event debrief, and whilst there was a lot of conversation around the operational and technical sides of the virtual conference, what Pascal felt compelled to point out was the rather unbecoming and disrespectful attitude of a large proportion of the audience.

- The late arrivals who then waste everyone's time asking questions about what they have missed

- The angry lady writing lengthy emails accompanied by physical outbursts while on camera

- The amateur athlete eating spoonsful of milk-drenched cereals all day long

- The enigmatic hooded figure, his masked face propped on his right hand

- The 'I am really busy' guy who spent most of the sessions speaking on the phone

- The proud house decorator who saw fit to take their laptop around their house (I guess to show us around) and give everyone motion sickness

- The online ordering addict who received many parcels that day and proceeded to open them in front of their webcam

And how could any of the attendees forget the dark silhouette of the woman with her back to her window, stroking a cat? The event had been a particularly unfortunate experience for Pascal, and as he told me this story, I felt compelled to ask him:

"Do you think the attendees realised they were representing themselves and their businesses to their future customers and advocates?"

While Pascal's experience as event emcee might be hair-raising, I'm willing to bet you've experienced some (if not all) of the above behaviours in the last virtual event you attended.

It goes without saying: don't be that person!

Here are some things to consider so you can demonstrate professionalism and be effective at attending virtual business events.

Before The Virtual Event

Just like attending in-person networking, plan ahead before attending any virtual event. Check the event's schedule and make a note of the sessions you want to attend and the people you want to meet. Prioritise those sessions and those people that align with your business goals. Be organised. Set a reminder on your calendar and make sure you log in a few minutes early to avoid any technical difficulties.

Test Your Technology
Technical glitches can be a significant setback when attending virtual events but are easily avoided. As a fellow geek I shouldn't have to tell you this, but check you have a stable internet connection and your devices are fully charged. Make sure you test your technology ahead of time, including your webcam and microphone.

Also, make sure you have a backup plan in case of any technical difficulties.

For instance, as a frequent speaker at virtual events, I've made sure I can quickly jump onto a tethered mobile connection on my smartphone or use a mobile broadband dongle connection, should my main broadband internet connection go down.

We've all been frustrated by being on time for a virtual event only for one of the other people in the meeting to experience issues with their tech. Don't be that person! It's so simple to avoid, providing you plan ahead.

Have a Dedicated Workspace

Having a dedicated workspace will help you stay focused and engaged during the event. Whether you're at home or in the office, choose a quiet and well-lit area with minimal distractions. If you're in the office, this might mean closing the door or, if you work in an open-plan environment, using headphones or putting up a 'Do Not Disturb' sign.

Make sure your workspace is organised and clutter-free. You don't want to be distracted by paperwork or half-finished cups of tea!

Likewise, turn off your app notifications. You wouldn't have your smartphone beeping, nor would you be expected to respond to emails during a conference (or perhaps you would, in which case you and I need to have a conversation about focusing your attention!). Take the same attitude into a virtual event and focus on the speakers and sessions.

It also goes without saying that if you haven't already, invest in suitable equipment. Having a comfortable chair and desk is essential for your comfort during the event.

Spend time setting up your computer and webcam correctly and test them thoroughly using Pascal's 'Contrast-Clutter-Clarity' formula. In other words: Can the audience see me correctly? What is in the background? Can they hear properly? Do a test recording and watch and listen to the footage whilst making notes about what you need to adjust.

Goals and Mapping

According to Pascal, by far the most grounding and practical activity before any virtual event is to compile a list with your goals, your questions and the solutions you seek, and to map those against the agenda of the virtual event. For example:

- **Business strategy:** What are the current obstacles hindering our business growth? What are the questions I need answering to overcome these hurdles?

- **Sales strategy:** Who are my ideal customers and who could introduce me to them? What questions could I ask to get feedback on our products and services?

- **Content strategy:** What are my plans for the future and who could I invite as contributors? What kind of content could I curate and share to my network?

- **Personal development strategy:** What skills do I want to develop? What do I want to be able to understand better and do better?

You should then match your need for clarity and guidance with the speakers and attendees taking part in the online event. Read the agenda thoroughly, follow the event's official social media accounts and hashtags, etc. and become one of the sharpest business detectives in your sector!

Each time you find an individual or organisation who is a match against one of your questions and goals, enter their details into that extra column. As a result, you are mapping the theme of the event and key individuals against what you want to get out of your investment in taking part.

This mapping exercise is great fun to undertake and will completely change how you feel about and relate to the virtual event and the people taking part.

Mindset and Posture
Now you have all that additional information, including individuals' LinkedIn profiles and more, you can start to build up anticipation for you and for your future connections.

You should begin by announcing on social media that you will be attending the virtual event, and highlighting what you are most looking forward to. Don't forget to thank in advance the organisers and speakers.

You might also share content produced by the speakers and participants, start asking questions and invite other participants to get in touch with you.

During The Virtual Event

Virtual events can be challenging to engage in since there is no physical presence. However, you can still participate by asking questions, sharing your thoughts and engaging with other attendees.

Again, be mindful of your attention. Turn off notifications, so you aren't tempted to go and check out that email.

Importantly, let's talk about posture and the message it conveys to others. The ideal is what is known as the news desk framing, whereby the newsreader can be seen comfortably sitting at their desk or standing up with little to no distraction, looking directly into the camera lens. That is the best way to communicate professionalism, focus and credibility for you and your brand. So, no more webcams up noses and no slouching!

During the event, remember that, unlike in-person events, you're staring at a screen, so use your virtual event break-time properly. Don't swap staring at one screen for another by using the break to scroll social media or browse your smartphone messages. Instead, manage your energy. Stand up, move around, take toilet breaks and make time to drink and eat during virtual event intermissions.

Finally, use the chat feature to ask questions or comment on the discussion. You can often join breakout rooms and network with other attendees during these events, and you should take advantage of these features.

As with in-person business networking events, you get out of them what you put into them!

Take Notes
Taking notes during virtual events is just as important as at physical events. It helps you retain information and refer to it later. While the temptation is to make notes on a digital device, you can easily get distracted by apps or notifications. Therefore, I prefer to take notes with good old-fashioned pen and paper, and then digitise those notes afterwards for reference purposes.

I highly recommend checking out Rocketbook reusable digital notebooks (https://tubb.co/rocketbook), which allow you to make handwritten notes and then quickly scan them into your second-brain apps such as Evernote or OneNote.

Whatever method you use, make sure you note down key takeaways, actionable insights and any questions you have.

After the Virtual Event

After the virtual event, follow up with the speakers or attendees you connected with in much the same way as you would for an in-person event, as we explored earlier. You can send a thank-you email, connect on social media, or schedule a follow-up call.

As with in-person business networking, following up promptly after a virtual event will help you build long-lasting relationships and open up new opportunities.

Post-Event Celebration

This final phase, often overlooked, is all about creating your own luck and maximising the value of your investment in participating in the online event.

Share your thoughts on social media, tagging all the speakers and organisers.

Create a social media carousel with a photo of each speaker per slide, together with your favourite advice and action point – and don't forget to give the organisers and attendees a shout-out.

Surprise the organisers and the speakers with an invitation to join you on a video and/or audio podcast to reflect on the event and expand upon their key messages. This is great content that you can repurpose in so many different formats and lengths!

> I firmly believe that there is no such thing as 'Zoom Fatigue' although I would agree that there can be 'Zoom Laziness' or 'Zoom Unpreparedness'.
>
> Pascal Fintoni

Summary

Attending virtual business events requires planning, focus and engagement.

- Before the event: set up a dedicated workspace, remove distractions and test your technology.

- During the event: dress and behave professionally, take handwritten notes and engage with speakers and other attendees via the chat function or breakout rooms.

- After the event: follow up with speakers, attendees and other contacts you've met. Thank the event organisers for their efforts.

Business Networking is a Skill

You'll have noticed that I've used the phrase "People do business with people they know, like and trust" several times throughout this book. That's because it's something to bear in mind with every interaction with someone, whether that's online or face to face.

Business owners need to make sure people know them, because you can have the greatest IT business in the world, but if nobody knows who you are, you won't achieve the success you want.

In his 2001 book *Dot.Bomb*, Rory Cellan-Jones explained how the success of some businesses during the peak of the dot.com bubble was down to a particular skill. "In the dot.com world, the key skill was not the ability to write elegant software, or understand the latest microprocessor architecture, or even draw up a convincing business plan. It was the people who knew how to network who stood the best chance…"

We've looked at traditional and social networking and concluded that doing one without the other isn't making full use of the tools at your disposal.

The MSP business I used to run was built on the back of strong relationships. And my current role as The IT Business Growth Expert keeps me busy through, in large part, the many strong business relationships I've formed in the past.

As a result of being a connector and treating your business contacts with respect, you can earn high levels of trust and confidence – which lasts for a long time.

Make no mistake about it, building relationships – be they with your prospective client base, strategic alliance partners, vendors or peers – isn't a 'nice to do, but only if you have time' activity. Instead, you should remember that business is done between people who know, like and trust one another. As a result, business relationships should be top of your priority list, and acting with respect and kindness to others part of your business DNA.

Attending business networking events and using social (online) networking isn't something to think about once you've done everything else that's important in your business. I believe building relationships is something you should be doing all the time, every day, as part of your standard day-to-day business activities.

> **Become That Interesting Person.** In the end, building your personal brand is about growing not your business, but yourself. You will learn to share and communicate better. You will also learn to identify and run with your own personal strengths. Are you a good orator? Do you tell stories well? Do you use analogies effectively? Are you funny? Find your strengths and challenge your weaknesses. And – unlike traditional business branding, where consistency is critical – personal branding is about growth and change. What could be more fun than this?
>
> Joshua Liberman, Net Sciences

In the next chapter, I want to look briefly at an overlooked part of business networking –leveraging the power of networking with your existing clients.

Bringing Your Clients Together Through Networking

By this stage, you'll probably have realised that being a 'connector' – someone who makes introductions that will be mutually beneficial to both parties – is something I think is a superpower for any geek looking to grow their business or career. But when it comes to being a connector, most people think of attending business networking events, using social networking, and finding new connections for your own business.

However, have you considered the power in the network you have already built within your client base?

Building Your Own Networking Event

On a number of occasions, I've arranged a networking session for clients of mine who are all attending the same conference. We usually schedule these get-togethers the day before or the evening after the conference. This allows people to come into town for the event early or stay a little later. And every time I've put together a group of my clients in this way, the feedback from attendees has been positive.

We jokingly refer to these sessions as World Domination Summits. It simply started as an excuse to bring my clients together under one roof and introduce them to one another. At the first WDS I encouraged each participant to share their areas of speciality and expertise – and in the weeks and months that followed that meeting I heard feedback from clients who were now collaborating on projects together and outsourcing specialist work to each other.

As the WDS events went on, I encouraged each participant to share their biggest challenges and most inspiring recent successes. I've been able to watch as everyone in the room learned by sharing experiences with each other, and every person came away with ideas to take back to their own business.

> At its heart, networking is about giving: giving your time, your expertise and your opportunities; keeping awareness within your clients of opportunities that may arise and knowing who you could introduce to help that client. The outcome of this approach is that you get the benefit of helping the client find a quality supplier and your networking buddy will then be looking out for opportunities for you, given they want to reciprocate the kindness.
>
> I've met people over the years in business via networking and kept in touch, worked with them and received opportunities. In one specific case someone in this category provided me with an opportunity which to this day remains one of the largest clients I've worked with from an income perspective. Had I not built and maintained this relationship then when the time came for him to find someone who could take some clients off his hands, I would not have received the call that led to that meeting, which led to taking on the client seven years ago.
>
> Craig Sharp, Abussi

Frankly, I'm the first to admit I wasn't actually needed in the room – gather together a bunch of the smartest and most progressive IT business owners in the UK, and all they really need is the slightest nudge from me as a facilitator to start talking to each other and the good ideas start flowing.

Which begs the question, if bringing your clients together through networking is valuable – why aren't more businesses doing it?

My clients are the owners of IT companies, but this concept works equally well with any type of business. You'll find that if you organise a networking event with your own clients – regardless of which industry they work in – they will find common ground. Everyone in the room benefits from the collected experience; it really produces a 'mastermind'-like effect for all concerned.

Have some fun with these events!

> We support our local football club, IT Wise, and often take friends, colleagues, customers – generally a mix – to a box to have a meal and watch the football. I invited a very old friend from primary school once who I hadn't seen in years. A week later, a £35k contract from the business his wife worked in arrived, just through a last-minute introduction. They are still customers today, and it wasn't even them who came to the box!
>
> David Brereton, Myson Pages

Bringing Your Own Clients Together

As an IT business, I'm positive that you have more than one client who you'd consider progressive in their ideas, successful in their execution of these ideas, and eager to build relationships with and learn from others. So why not start introducing your customers or clients to one another and help nurture those relationships?

If those clients help one another, their respective businesses will grow as a result – all of which is good for you as their partner too!

What's more, don't underestimate the value business owners place on maintaining a relationship with the connectors of this world. If your client sees you as someone who knows and can connect them with other positive, successful business owners, they'll value their relationship with you all the more.

Putting on your own World Domination Summit might be something to plan ahead for. All you need is a room, a few pots of tea or coffee and some eager attendees. However, don't let logistics get in the way of starting to connect your clients immediately!

Have a think about your client list and what some of your clients may have in common. For example, they may be similarly sized businesses in like-minded but non-competitive areas of commerce. Or they may be experiencing the same challenges as one another: growth, recruitment, marketing, technology.

Once you've spoken to your clients to explain that you feel an introduction would be useful, and to ask their permission, you could send a simple email outlining why you're connecting the two business owners and what benefits you see them getting from this connection.

In my experience, the results provide even more value to my clients than I already do. As an IT business owner, how powerful might it be for you to connect your clients to one another?

> To network with our clients, we host our own 'CON' called T-CON (also short for T-Consulting, creativity at its best!), a format clients now recognise and anticipate.
>
> We bring them all under one roof for a whole day and provide information, awareness, technical labs, and one-on-one meetings with vendors around the topic of cybersecurity.
>
> Vera Tucci, T-Consulting

Summary

In this chapter we've explored how you benefit from bringing your existing clients together to help them network.

- Look for opportunities to be the connector and introduce your clients to one another.

- Build your own business networking event where you invite existing clients to attend and meet one another.

- Consider piggybacking your event onto a conference or trade show that other people are already planning to attend.

Now we've looked at the various types of networking available to you, and how to get the most out of them, let's feed your inner geek by looking at some of the techie tools that are available to help you network more effectively!

Digital Business Card Apps to Make Networking and Follow-ups Easier

In an earlier chapter, I shared with you the importance of setting aside time to effectively record information about new contacts in your system, and then follow up effectively. I mentioned that you could use simple notes in your Outlook or Google Contacts, or investigate using a Professional Services Automation (PSA) or Customer Relationship Management (CRM) system to capture this information.

However, there is now an abundance of tools you can use to streamline this process. Here are some of my recommendations for apps you can use during networking events, meetings and conferences, and to make following up and connecting with your new contacts even easier. You'll find all the links in the resources section at the end of the chapter.

Haystack (iOS, Android)

Haystack is an app that allows you to scan traditional business cards and exchange your own electronic business card with others – in effect, it provides you with a digital business card and a business card scanner in one app.

While there are plenty of business card scanning apps on the market, this one has impressed me with its ability to accurately scan in all the contact details from a physical business card (including company logos) and add it to your contacts list with ease.

Additionally, the app makes it easy to send your own digital business card to any new contacts. If you've ever run out of physical cards at a conference or networking event, this app turns your blushes into an opportunity to demonstrate some new tech!

Haystack is free for individual use, with a premium paid option offering corporate templates and more features for larger organisations.

CamCard (iOS, Android)

I've also used CamCard to scan business cards and automatically input them into my contact list. It's available for Android and iOS and is actually very strong at OCR (Optical Character Recognition). Once you've scanned the card in, CamCard keeps a handy history of the cards you've scanned for when you need a reminder of who you've met and where.

Speaking of which, once you've scanned the person's contact details into your contact list, make sure you use the Notes section to write where you met them and the memory hooks you recorded (as mentioned earlier – what you spoke about, who introduced you, etc.). These are invaluable later when you can't remember somebody's name but can remember the details of the meeting.

Covve (iOS, Android)

I've found Covve to be very useful in prompting me to follow up with people. It not only scans business cards and stores your contacts, but it also helps you maintain your relationships with these contacts. Once you've scanned and saved a contact, you can take advantage of the auto-remind option so you can set a timer for how often you want to reach out to someone.

Blinq (iOS, Android)

Blinq allows you to instantly share who you are with anyone, wherever you go. Using QR code technology, your Blinq digital business card can be easily shared with anyone you meet even if they don't have the app. With Blinq you can share your logo, profile picture, job title, company name, headline, email address, phone numbers, links and more.

When you receive a digital business card, Blinq automatically logs when and where you met your new contact. You can also add notes to your cards to record key details, so Blinq is a great way to allow you to capture lots of key information that you might otherwise forget!

Evernote / OneNote

If you use a 'second brain' application such as Evernote or OneNote, there are facilities within these applications to scan and recognise business cards. For instance, Microsoft Office Lens has a business card scanner built in, and Evernote Scannable allows you to take a photo of a business card as a note and then Evernote will store the photo as a business card.

Business Cards Aren't Dead… Yet!

While apps such as LinkedIn are becoming an increasingly popular way to connect with people without using physical business cards, I would still recommend you use an app or build a process for dealing with cards.

Why? Well, a digital-only approach may work for you, but rest assured there are many people who prefer old school business cards!

After all, remember my tip about writing memory hooks on the back of the business cards you collect? Sometimes whipping your smartphone out during a conversation isn't appropriate, whereas taking a pen out to write something is more socially acceptable.

Remember, the point here is to connect and follow up with people in a timely fashion. You don't want a desk full of business cards gathering dust!

> I know we live in a digital world but have a good business card.
>
> And if someone gives you a business card, compliment it positively. Maybe the details, the look, or the feel. They'll smile when you compliment them, and they're more likely to remember you.
>
> Robert Gibbons, IT Expert

Resources

- Haystack: https://tubb.co/haystack
- CamCard: https://tubb.co/camcard
- Covve: https://covve.com/
- Bling: https://blinq.me/
- Evernote: https://tubb.co/evernote
- OneNote: https://www.microsoft.com/en-us/microsoft-365/onenote/digital-note-taking-app

The Importance of Peer Groups

In the fast-paced world of IT, MSPs and IT solution providers face a multitude of challenges on a daily basis. As a former MSP myself, I know that IT businesses need to manage complex networks, keep up with the latest technology trends and always respond in a timely fashion to ever-changing client requests. In short, the demands of the IT industry can be overwhelming.

In an earlier chapter, we discussed how tough it can be to be an IT professional or run your own IT business. And in one of my earlier books, *The IT Business Owner's Survival Guide*, I urged IT professionals like you not to try to make this journey on your own – because if you do, the journey can be a lonely and stressful one.

However, one way MSPs can find support and stay ahead of the curve is by attending peer groups. My own MSP business was built off the back of participating in these. They are usually a good place to meet and make contact with people with whom you share an interest. There are peer groups focused around the Managed Services industry as a whole, and peer groups dedicated to individual technologies such as Microsoft 365, Azure and Amazon Web Services.

As an IT business owner, it's usually a good idea to attend local groups that share an interest in business, IT or both. For example, I've already mentioned The Tech Tribe, an awesome community for MSPs. Well, in recent years, I was part of an initiative to bring local, in-person Tech Tribe meetups to the UK. As a result, there are now monthly Tech Tribe meetups all across the United Kingdom, with new groups springing up in Europe, Australia and North America, too. At the end of this chapter, I'll list some resources to help you find peer groups near you.

> How do you approach building relationships with new contacts in your industry? Be part of it – I think it is that simple. Get involved with peer groups, attend events, listen, and join in. Before you know it, you are part of the community, and it's a uniquely open and sharing place. Yes, we are all competitors, but until there isn't enough work to go around, you'll rarely find you are ever in competition.
>
> David Brereton, Myson Pages

The idea of a peer group is to help everyone who attends to better run their business. These groups allow you to share your ideas on relevant topics, discuss new trends and ask questions that others may be able to help with. In some cases, you can build business relationships with people who are lacking a skill or discipline that you may be able to provide, or vice versa.

The collaboration opportunities that peer groups provide can help you solve problems you may have in your business or tap into new resources. For example, if recruitment for your business is a problem, one of your peers at the group might be able to recommend a recruitment company that they've had a degree of success with.

As well as building personal relationships with the organisers and attendees, these groups help you build a community network of business owners who are likely to have a range of further contacts that they might be willing to introduce you to. In fact, I sold my MSP business to a business owner I met through a peer group! This sale happened because the buyer (James) and I got to know, like and trust each other as a result of our interactions in the group. So, when I made the decision to exit my IT business, the sales cycle was dramatically shortened thanks to the investment James and I had already made in the group.

And if you think I'm alone in this story, let my friend Pete Matheson share how he sold his business through a peer group connection, too!

> I signed up to the Tech Tribe for one purpose: to download all the available resources, which I needed, then cancel my membership, never to be seen again! 😂
>
> Instead, what I found was an unashamedly helpful community of IT business owners who were helping each other with their business challenges. Taking time out of their already hectic days to help and support others.
>
> A few short months later, I ended up posting an anonymous question to the Tech Tribe community, asking if there would be any interest in acquiring my MSP, as I was considering selling.
>
> Fast forward three months, and I'd sold my MSP to someone I was introduced to via the Tech Tribe forums.
>
> I'd like to give my personal thanks to Nigel for creating such a wonderful community.
>
> Pete Matheson, MSP Business Coach and Mentor

Peer groups can build an incredible amount of trust and some really valuable connections.

But the benefits don't end there! So, as an IT business, what other benefits can you expect to realise from participating in a peer group?

Networking Opportunities

Given that this is a book about business networking, I have to lead by saying that one of the most significant benefits of attending peer groups is the networking opportunities they provide. By interacting with other MSPs and technology businesses, you can expand your professional network and develop relationships with other professionals in the industry. You can also learn about the latest technology trends, share best practices, and gain new insights into your business. Plus, you can build what are known as 'strategic alliances'.

I'm a huge fan of strategic alliances. Simply put, your IT business can 'buddy up' with other technology businesses to provide complementary services to your clients. After all, you can't be an expert in everything. Therefore, building up relationships with other businesses (some examples include data cablers, VoIP providers, SharePoint, CRM or Linux specialists, plus many others) allows you to provide solutions and services for your clients that you might not otherwise be able to.

> You will encounter competitors in the informal networking groups. Don't shy away from them. They could have interesting insights about the local market and could end up being useful strategic partners. We met a residential IT specialist this way to whom we have been able to pass all our former residential customers and new enquiries rather than leaving them in the lurch. Hopefully he will eventually feel obliged to reciprocate with an opportunity that does not fit his business model, although there's no guarantee of this.
>
> Suzanne Rice, Computer Troubleshooters

Knowledge Sharing

Peer groups provide a platform for knowledge sharing. Through networking with other MSPs and technology providers, you can access valuable information that can help you improve your business operations. For example, you can learn about new software tools, techniques for managing networks, and effective ways to market your business.

And if you're concerned about sharing knowledge with your so-called competitors, then please don't worry. The old adage about "A rising tide lifts all boats" is absolutely true in the IT industry and I've never come across an industry where so many people are willing to help one another out. There are more than enough clients for everybody, so you don't need to worry about your competitors stealing a march on you – that is, unless you don't attend peer groups and hear the latest information they are hearing!

Business Growth

With that said, by attending peer groups, you can gain insights into how other MSPs are growing their businesses. You can learn about new revenue streams, innovative pricing models, and effective sales strategies. This information can help you identify new opportunities for growth and make better decisions for your business.

As a result of attending peer groups, one of the key areas that I developed for my MSP business was which vendors to partner with, and which tools to use (and which to avoid).

As I've mentioned numerous times already, the best recommendations come from those who have been there and done that – and you can find this information at a peer group.

Professional Development

By reading this book, I know you're somebody who wants to develop professionally.

Therefore, please know that peer groups provide a valuable opportunity for professional development. You can attend training sessions, workshops and seminars on a variety of topics related to the IT industry. By staying up to date with the latest trends and technologies, you can enhance your skills and provide better services to your clients.

> Networking partners or mentors – work out who's the best for you. It might not be the obvious person or industry.
>
> A secret – mine is a person whose business supplies services to the legal sector, particularly conveyancing departments. Think outside the box. 😉
>
> Robert Gibbons, IT Expert

Industry Advocacy

Peer groups can also be a powerful tool for industry advocacy. By working together, MSPs can advocate for policies and regulations that support the industry. They can also raise awareness about the benefits of MSP services and the value they provide to businesses. For example, CompTIA (https://www.comptia.org) is a worldwide organisation that offers peer groups and advocacy for the IT industry.

In conclusion, attending peer groups is a valuable investment for IT MSPs. They provide networking opportunities, knowledge sharing, business growth, professional development, and industry advocacy. By participating in peer groups, you can stay ahead of the curve, develop new skills, and provide a better service for your clients.

So, where can you find peer groups that are relevant to your IT business and geography?

Well, I asked our very own Stephen McCormick, MSP Community

Manager at Tubblog - The Hub for MSPs, which peer groups he recommends.

Stephen spends a lot of his time visiting peer groups and spending time with IT businesses. He says he has discovered that people at peer groups are often eager to be helpful, but membership can vary. Therefore, it's worth attending a few different peer groups to find one or two that suit you best.

While there are dozens of peer groups for IT businesses worldwide, here are three peer groups you might want to consider.

> **Learn From Peers.** One of the great shortcuts to achieving proficiency in any craft is to learn from others. To that end, I have chosen to participate in three types of groups. Membership groups such as The ASCII Group, Karl Palachuk's Small Business Thoughts, and Tech Tribe are top of the list. Next come peer groups for sharing of challenges, ideas, and commiseration.
>
> Joining partner advisory councils is a way to learn, share, and even direct their decision making as well, if you get lucky. I have also chosen to embrace writing in the industry, for vendors, peer groups and ChannelPro magazine, primarily. There is a bonus in all of this. I get to travel more, make friends worldwide and 'climb different rocks' as well.
>
> Joshua Liberman, Net Sciences

The Tech Tribe

The Tech Tribe is one of the world's most loved communities to help you run an MSP or IT service provider business. Founded by former MSP owner Nigel Moore, the Tribe is an awesome online community for Managed Service Providers.

But the Tech Tribe is no longer just an online peer group! As I mentioned, you can now visit local Tech Tribe meetups across the world. What's more, you don't need to be a member of The Tech Tribe to attend these local Tribal meetups!

CompTIA Business Technology Community

The aforementioned CompTIA organisation is a global non-profit dedicated to raising the bar of professionalism within the IT industry. You might be familiar with CompTIA from their IT certifications, such as the A+ certification. However, they also run a series of worldwide peer groups and communities that members can attend to swap ideas, information and best practice.

ConnectWise IT Nation Evolve

IT Nation Evolve is an annual membership programme designed to help you navigate your business journey through peer group interactions. Unlike the other peer groups we've mentioned here, IT Nation Evolve is a more intimate setting where groups of a dozen MSPs get together to help one another grow.

As a former member of IT Nation Evolve (or HTG, as it was known back then) with my MSP, I can attest to the value in these smaller peer groups. There is a high degree of accountability and business-focused growth strategies.

The investment of time and money in peer groups like IT Nation Evolve can put some IT businesses off, but those who participate experience exceptional returns on the investment they've made.

> One effective way we promote our company is by being part of different business groups.
>
> My partner and I have prominent roles within a national business association, a local IT vertical council, and a regional business network that aims to generate innovative ideas. Being recognised as leading actors in the innovation world benefits the authority we want to express with our company.
>
> Sitting on different boards allows us to share our vision and approach without actively pitching it. The results have been great so far because this goes beyond 'word of mouth'. Decision-makers can interact with us personally and learn to trust us in a neutral, friendly environment. It's like a business relationship sandbox!
>
> Vera Tucci, T-Consulting

Summary

In this chapter, we've explored why peer groups are such a powerful way for you to grow your business.

- Peer groups can provide you with networking opportunities, the chance to share and receive knowledge and experience business growth.
- Peer groups are a great method of personal development.
- Industry advocacy is a wider benefit of peer groups and helps raise the bar of professionalism for your business as well as your peers.
- A rising tide lifts all boats. Don't be afraid of collaborating with so-called competitors.

- Attendees at peer groups are often eager to be helpful, but be aware that membership can vary. It is worth attending a few different peer groups to find one or two that suit you best.

Further Resources

- Article: The Power of Help Through Your Local MSP Peer Groups - https://tubb.co/peergrouppower
- List: A List of User Groups for UK Managed Service Providers - https://tubb.co/msppeergroups
- For more details of The Tech Tribe, visit http://www.tubblog.co.uk/TechTribe/
- For more details about The Tech Tribe Local Gatherings, visit https://tubb.co/techtribelocal
- Listen to my interview with the illustrious leader of the Tech Tribe, Nigel Moore, in TubbTalk 51: Building The Tech Tribe for MSPs (https://www.tubblog.co.uk/podcasts/building-the-tech-tribe-for-msps/)
- For more details on CompTIA, visit https://www.comptia.org
- For more details on the CompTIA IT communities, visit https://connect.comptia.org/connect/communities
- For more details on IT Nation Evolve, visit https://www.connectwise.com/theitnation/evolve
- Check out my interview with Dan Scott in TubbTalk 117: How to Grow Your Business in an MSP Community Like IT Nation (https://www.tubblog.co.uk/podcasts/grow-business-msp-community/)
- Listen to my interview with HTG (now IT Nation Evolve) founder Arlin Sorensen in TubbTalk 29: Why Discipline and Planning are Vital to Success in Business and Life (https://www.tubblog.co.uk/podcasts/discipline-and-planning-are-vital/)

IT Conferences and Their Importance to Your Business

I think it is fair to say that Information Technology has transformed businesses across industries, making it an essential component of the modern enterprise. The IT Managed Service Provider industry, in particular, is rapidly evolving, and as we've already explored, staying up to date with the latest trends and developments is crucial for success.

In addition to attending peer groups, one of the most effective ways for IT MSPs to stay informed and connected with the industry is by attending IT conferences. These provide MSPs with a unique opportunity to network, learn and collaborate with industry peers, experts and vendors. The conferences I have attended over the years have offered an array of benefits, including access to the latest technologies, insights from industry experts and opportunities to build relationships that can lead to new business.

While I know from experience that stepping away from your day-to-day in order to attend conferences can be a big investment of time and money, I will say that it is one of the fastest ways to grow.

The Benefits of Attending IT Conferences

So, what are the benefits of you attending conferences?

Staying current with industry trends and best practices
IT conferences provide an excellent opportunity to learn about the latest trends, best practices, and emerging technologies that are shaping the industry. By attending sessions and interacting with peers, you can gain valuable insights into new developments and

techniques, which you can then use to improve your services and stay ahead of the competition.

> Networking with people in related businesses can often lead to beneficial opportunities. In related but not directly competing businesses you can often pass opportunities between you which help all parties. Examples of this are the IT/web/telecoms industries where one person may be approached to offer a service but can't, and so would be happy to work with you to deliver it, or to hand it over.
>
> In the past, I have received opportunities from telecom companies who were able to complete part of a requirement but needed an IT element bolted on; a partnership that would only be possible by building relationships through networking.
>
> Craig Sharp, Abussi

Access to industry experts and thought leaders
IT conferences attract some of the most prominent names in the industry, including technology vendors, consultants, and thought leaders. By attending these events, you can gain access to these experts, learn from their experiences, and get valuable advice on how to navigate challenges and grow your business.

Networking opportunities
Of course, in a book about business networking, we must address the huge benefits networking at a conference brings your business! Conferences are an excellent opportunity for you to network with peers, experts and vendors, providing a platform for MSPs to connect with other like-minded professionals, build relationships and explore potential business partnerships. Networking at these events can lead to new business opportunities, partnerships and collaborations that can help your IT business to grow.

I should add that just like at business networking events, some of the best networking that happens at IT conferences happens outside the halls and inside the coffee shops, bars and restaurants. Don't restrict your networking to the official schedule – get involved in the events surrounding the event!

> We choose national and international peer events, usually hosted by vendors or distributors, to continuously improve our MSP. These events – especially when they require travelling abroad – can be expensive and take you out of the office for many days, but they are vital for the business.
>
> My advice for those at the beginning of the journey is, even if you think you can't attend right now, ask yourself "Why?" and look for a solution!
>
> Is it a 'financial why'? Use the event's website to look for familiar vendors: they might be willing to support your participation with a complimentary pass. Or reach out to the organisers via LinkedIn and ask if they plan to broadcast the event or have alternatives closer to you. Worst case, you made a good business connection and will still be part of the conversation around the event.
>
> If it's an '"operational why' and you're worried about missing too many work days, plan ahead your workload. This way – even if you won't be completely free – you might be able to focus on specific tasks that can be done remotely throughout the day (also without the office or home distractions!).
>
> Vera Tucci, T-Consulting

Access to new technologies

IT conferences often showcase the latest technologies, products and services that are shaping the industry. Attending these events provides you with the opportunity to explore these new technologies and learn about their potential applications in your business. By staying up to date with the latest technologies, you can offer your clients the most innovative solutions, which can help them (and you!) stay ahead of the competition.

Inspiration and motivation

Attending IT conferences can be a source of inspiration and motivation for both you as a leader, and your business as a whole. These events provide a platform for you to connect with peers and industry leaders, share their experiences, and learn from others. As we discussed in our chapter on peer groups, by interacting with like-minded professionals, you can gain new perspectives and ideas, which can help you grow your business and reach your goals.

Summary

In this chapter we have explored why you should invest the time and money to attend IT industry conferences and other events.

- Conferences are an excellent opportunity for you to network with peers, experts and vendors.

- IT conferences provide an excellent opportunity to learn about the latest trends, best practices, and emerging technologies that are shaping the industry.

- Attending IT conferences can be a source of inspiration and motivation for you and your business.

- Don't restrict your networking to the official schedule – some of the best networking happens outside the halls and inside the coffee shops, bars and restaurants.

Further Resources

Attending IT conferences is essential for MSPs who want to stay competitive and grow their business. If you're on the lookout for some IT events to attend, then look no further! Check out the List of Awesome Events for MSPs at https://tubb.co/mspevents

Conclusion

Throughout this book, we've explored themes of business relationships. The old adage that "People do business with people they know, like and trust" has never been more true than today.

Despite the rise in social media, business networking has continued to thrive, both at in-person business networking events and conferences and via social networking. Business networking is one of the most important aspects of building and growing a successful IT business. It's a valuable strategy that can help IT businesses of all sizes and IT professionals of all experience levels to connect with potential clients, partners and industry experts.

For techy geeks like us, business networking can offer a range of benefits that can help us build our brand, attract new clients, and stay ahead of the competition. It's an effective way to generate new leads and sales and by attending networking events, conferences and meetups, you can connect with potential clients and partners who are interested in your services.

However, remember that you can't jump straight to the sales – you first need to allow people to get to know you, like you and trust you. Networking allows you to establish those personal relationships with a wide range of people, including potential clients, which can lead to new business opportunities.

Business networking is also an excellent way to build brand awareness. By attending events and meeting other business owners, you can increase your visibility and establish yourself as an expert in your field. This can help to build trust and credibility with potential clients, which can lead to more business in the future.

As one geek to another, I hope this book has allowed you to view networking with fresh eyes, step outside your comfort zone and realise that business networking is not dissimilar to computer networking – you just have to understand how it works before jumping in.

I'd love to hear your feedback and continue the conversation.

Visit Tubblog - The Hub for MSPs at https://www.tubblog.co.uk or do a quick search for 'Richard Tubb MSP' and get in touch with me directly.

Happy networking!

Business Networking Event Cheat Sheet

Keep this cheat sheet in mind to remind you of a system you can use to succeed at business networking.

I've made it available as a downloadable PDF on my website at www.tubblog.co.uk.

Before The Event

- Choose the right event. Check with your business contacts to see which events they recommend.

- Check out the attendee list to see who else is attending the event, and go into the event with a plan.

- Announce you're attending the event on social media. Others may seek you out or even attend the event because you are going.

- Schedule time in your diary to process business cards and new connections after the event.

During The Event

- Look for an open conversation to join. Avoid closed groups.

- Actively listen. Make it all about them.

- Be the connector. Who else can you connect this person with that would be valuable to them?

- Write memory hooks on business cards to help you effectively follow up.

After The Event

- Process business cards and add new connections into your system.

- Connect with new contacts on LinkedIn and other social networking platforms.

- Email new contacts to follow up on any conversations or commitments.

- Be the connector again. Who else can you connect this person with that would be valuable to them?

- Send a video message to enable you to be remarkable and stand out from the crowd.

Acknowledgements

This book started out as an experiment, drawing on years of blog posts and other articles I've written for Tubblog - The Hub for MSPs and other websites.

A huge thank you to my friend and colleague Gudrun Lauret for suggesting this book and for helping me produce it.

Thank you to my friends and contributors to this book: Adam Foster, Craig Sharp, David Brereton, Dave Algeo, John Espirian, Joshua Liberman, Nigel Moore, Pete Matheson, Robert Gibbons, Stefan Thomas, Stephen McCormick, Suzanne Rice and Vera Tucci. You are all world-class experts that I've learned from and people I have a great deal of admiration for. I hope this book helps others learn from your wisdom, too.

To my main man Col Gray for designing the book cover, Michael de Groot for organising the wonderful geek-themed illustrations, and to The Proof Fairy, Alison Thompson, for once again helping me turn this book into a publishable volume!

I'd also like to thank my colleagues at Team Tubb – for their support and guidance, without which I'd never have been able to make the time or find the energy to finish this book.

To my friend and mentor, Pascal Fintoni, thank you for all your support, inspiration and motivation. I appreciate you, mon ami.

To my coach, Rob Hatch. I value your support and wisdom more than you know.

And to my family – my wife Claire for her love and support, my stepchildren Ben and Ryan for being loveable idiots who make me laugh, and to my Mom, Bruv and Sis for always having my back.

Printed in Great Britain
by Amazon